Going Beyond
Buddha

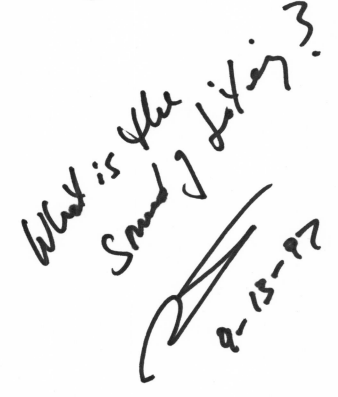

What is the
Sound of living?

a-13-97

Going Beyond Buddha

The Awakening Practice of Listening

Zen Master Dae Gak

Charles E. Tuttle Co., Inc.
Boston • Rutland, Vermont • Tokyo

First published in 1997 by Charles E. Tuttle Publishing, an imprint of Periplus Editions (HK) Ltd., with editorial offices at 153 Milk Street, Boston, Massachusetts 02109.

Text on pages 10–14 is from the Surangama Sutra, translated by Dwight Goddard from *A Buddhist Bible* by Dwight Goddard, Editor. Copyright 1938, renewed © 1966 by E. P. Dutton. Used by permission of Dutton Signet, a division of Penguin Books USA, Inc.

The calligraphy on page vi is "No-hole Flute" by Seung Sahn. The enso on page xvi is by Dae Gak. The illustration on page 141 is by Melissa Kelley.

Library of Congress Cataloging-in-Publication Data

Dae Gak, 1947—
    Going beyond Buddha : the awakening practice of listening / by Zen Master Dae Gak.
      p. cm.
    ISBN 0-8048-3116-5
    1. Spiritual life—Buddhism. 2. Listening—Religious aspects—
–Buddhism. I. Title.
BQ5660.D34 1997
294.3 ' 444—dc21   97—195
                                  CIP

Distributed by

USA	Japan
Charles E. Tuttle Co., Inc.	Tuttle Shokai Ltd.
RR 1 Box 231-5	1-21-13, Seki
North Clarendon,VT	Tama-ku, Kawasaki-shi 214
05759	Japan
(800) 526-2778	(044) 833-0225
Fax: (800) FAX-TUTL	Fax: (044) 822-0413

Southeast Asia
Berkeley Books Pte Ltd
5 Little Road #08-01
Singapore 536983
(65) 280-3320
Fax: (65) 280-6290

First Edition
05 04 03 02 01 00 99 98 97   1 3 5 7 9 10 8 6 4 2

Design by Fran Kay
Printed in the United States of America

Contents

Foreword

Listening practice means keeping a not-moving mind, perceiving your true self. Perceiving your true self means perceiving all sound just as it is. Perceiving sound just as it is means you and the Universe become one. You and the Universe become one; all suffering disappears, and complete stillness appears. This stillness is bliss. If you keep this mind, your mind becomes clear, clear like a mirror. When your mind is clear, everything is clear. Red comes: red. Blue comes: blue. Dog comes: "arf, arf." Someone comes who is hungry, give him food. Someone comes who is tired, give him a place to sleep. The name for this is Great Love, Great Compassion, Great Bodhisattva Way.

Many Zen masters' minds have opened hearing sound. One famous story is about Su Tong-Po. Su Tong-Po was a high official whose job was to investigate all government activities in the four provinces to which he was assigned. In addition to being a famous poet, he had memorized all the 84,000 Buddhist texts. Su Tong-Po enjoyed visiting many temples during his travels and questioning the nuns, monks, and masters as to their knowledge of the Buddhist teachings. No one could answer his questions to his satisfaction.

One day, Su Tong-Po heard of a great Zen master in the monastery in Jade Springs. During his next trip to that province, Su Tong-Po visited the temple. The master respectfully greeted the high official and asked him his name. Su Tong-Po replied, "Ch'eng" (*Ch'eng* means "scales") and quickly added, "because I measure all the eminent teachers in the land." Without hesitation, the Zen master shouted, "Katz!" and asked Su Tong-Po how much it weighed. The government official was speechless. A response to this question was not in any of the sutras that he had read. At that moment, Su Tong-Po devoted himself to Zen practice.

In search for the meaning of life and death, Su Tong-Po studied with many masters, including the famous Zen Master Chang Tsung. During one interview, Su Tong-Po asked Zen Master Chang Tsung to open up his ignorant ears and teach him the Buddha-dharma. The master became enraged and yelled, "How dare you come in here seeking the dead words of teachers! Why don't you open your ears to the living words of Nature? I can't talk to someone who knows so much about Zen. Go away!"

Su Tong-Po was stunned. He didn't know what to say or what to do. What had the master meant? Su Tong-Po bowed to the master and left. Mounting his horse, Su Tong-Po rode on a path that led him into the mountains. Suddenly, he came upon a waterfall, and the sound struck his ears. At the moment of listening to the sound of the waterfall, Su Tong-Po's mind opened. That evening, he composed the following poem:

The roaring waterfall
is the Buddha's golden speech.
The mountains in the distance
are the Buddha's pure luminous body.
How many thousands of poems
have flowed through me tonight!
And tomorrow I won't be able
to repeat even one word.

There is much suffering in this world. How can we help this world of suffering? That is most important! All sound is Universal Sound: birds singing, thunder crashing, water falling. When you perceive sound as it is, then your correct situation, correct relationship, correct function become clear. Then all your speech and your every action will help all beings.

Zen Master Dae Gak is a strong and clear teacher. For many years Dae Gak Sunim has been a psychologist and has helped many people. Now he is a great Zen master and he helps this whole world.

I hope everyone reads this book, realizes the mind of listening, finds their true self, and saves all sentient beings from suffering.

Blue mountain never moves.
Water flows to the ocean,
nonstop.

Seung Sahn
April 1997
Hwa Gye Sah Temple
Seoul, Korea

Preface

The Chinese master Dongshan once taught, "Concerning realization, through the body, of going beyond Buddha, I would like to talk a little." A monk said, "What is this talk?" Dongshan said, "When I talk, you don't hear it." The monk asked, "Can you hear it, Master?" Then Dongshan replied, "Wait until I don't talk, then you will hear it."

Listening is the fundamental practice of any spiritual path. By definition, "to listen" means to pay attention in order to hear, to heed, or to attend. In listening, we perceive things as they are. To perceive is to become one with our experience.

Becoming one is to manifest in the moment, alive and immediate. If our listening is partial, there is still an *I* who is listening, and our listening is tainted by this. It is only when listening is complete that the enlightened mind appears.

Listening as a practice can be a very direct way to take spiritual practice into everyday life. Because listening is a part of both the spiritual and the mundane realms, the barrier between "Zen" and life dissolves in listening practice. Zen practice is functional whether listening to the breath or listening to a friend complain, whether sitting in a temple or riding on a bus, while attending the most sacred ceremony or listening to the screech and clatter of a busy hospital emergency room. It takes no particular skill or understanding to listen. It only takes trying. So we say, Try, try, try for ten thousand years. Because we are humans, we are compassionate by nature. But our compassion becomes lost in self-interest. Listening is a practice that returns us to our true way. The way of human beings. The way of compassion.

Listening is a difficult practice. It takes enormous effort and intention to listen clearly. We are distracted and absorbed by the mind-habit of years of conditioning. This book encourages us to see through this mind-habit and grasp the immediacy of experience. We are always listening. We are listening now. We listen with our eyes; we listen with our nose, our tongue. We listen with every cell and every pore of our whole body.

This book is a composite of edited talks given during meditation retreats over the past seven years. Most were given at Furnace Mountain, a Zen retreat center in the mountains of eastern Kentucky. Furnace Mountain offers residential training and monthly sitting meditation retreats for residents and guests. In this book, there is also a talk from a Zen-Christian retreat. Each spring a retreat is held at the Abbey of Gethsemani, a Catholic monastery in Bardstown, Kentucky, where Thomas Merton lived. Both Buddhists and Catholic monks, nuns, and laypeople of all denominations come together for dialogue and practice.

Many of the teaching stories presented here are part of the classic oral Zen tradition. The author's re-telling of them is in no way intended to represent other published versions.

The author is indebted to many for their help in bringing this book to completion. Without the Buddha's awakening and the transmission of his teaching, without the countless teachers and students of the Way, there would be no Zen training. I am especially grateful to my teacher, Zen Master Seung Sahn Haeng Won, who came to America in 1972 and has given his Dharma freely to all who have come to hear it. I am also indebted to the lineage of Korean Zen masters who trace their heritage back to Shakyamuni Buddha, including Zen Master Seung Sahn's teacher, Zen Master Ko Bong; his teacher, Zen Master Man Gong, and his teacher, Zen Master Kyong Ho. I am grateful for the Kwan Um School of Zen and the sangha of Furnace Mountain, who have been steadfast and unswerving in their support and encouragement. There are many individuals who have typed, edited, and commented on this manuscript.

Kwang Myong Sunim, Ji Do Poep Sa, has been tireless in her commitment and effort to bring this manuscript to press. Joyce Janca-Aji has been a wonderful help in transcribing and editing. Hyon Do Sunim, Zen Master Wu Kwang, Zen Master Bo Mun, Mu Sang Su Nim, Michael Kerber, Lorette Zirker, and Debra Brown have all encouraged, supported, and given invaluable constructive criticism. I also want to thank Melissa Kelley for her wonderful drawing on page 141. I would like to thank my parents and my children, who have been unselfish in their listening. And finally, I want to thank Mara, whose steadfast commitment and love have not been limited by condition, opinion, or situation.

> *True perception has no root.*
> *Clear listening has no sound.*
> *When you hear the beat of hooves*
> *Don't say zebra, don't say horse.*
>
> *One ear appears*
> *all sounds appear.*
> *One ear disappears*
> *all sounds disappear.*
>
> *If you have ears*
> *I will hit you thirty times!*
> *If you have no ears*
> *I will hit you thirty times!*
>
> *Why!*
>
> *Katz!!*

The roar of the great river
transforms heaven and earth.
The bald eagle rises slowly, slowly, slowly
In the clear blue sky.
Aiee, Aiee . . . Aiee!

Dae Gak
Furnace Mountain
April 8, 1997

Chapter One

Listen

Introduction

During my training for a Ph.D. in clinical psychology, I interned for one year at the Cleveland Psychiatric Institute, a state mental hospital in Ohio. My job was to work with the resident schizophrenic patients.

There was a secretary who worked in the main office. In the morning, she would come in and sit in a chair, and she'd stay there all day long, typing away. She had been there for years, knew everything there was to know about hospital politics, and shared her knowledge willingly. Her office was two or three doors down from mine, and we became good friends during my time there.

The offices were small. Mine was five by ten feet. So it was quite close quarters. The office had a desk, a large window, and two wooden captain's chairs with slats in the back. The ceilings were quite high, perhaps twelve feet, so one had the sense of being in a column. I would sit, and the patient and I would be quite close, almost knee to knee in these wooden chairs in this little office. If you have ever worked with schizophrenia, if you have ever known a schizophrenic or been schizo-phrenic, you know that sitting knee to knee with some-body in a little office is not paradise.

There is an interpersonal tension that develops between patient and doctor in those circumstances. In this tension of intimacy, in this intrusion of personal space, psychotic persons are put under such great stress that their typical dysfunctional adaptive behavior be-comes exaggerated.

One day I was sitting with a woman who jerked and twitched as I tried to give her the Rorschach inkblot test. She asked me, "What is that noise?" I could hear nothing. It was silent.

She again insisted, "What is that noise? It is so loud in here! Can't you make them stop?"

I at once concluded that she was having an audi-tory hallucination, which is a key diagnostic sign of schizophrenia. She became more and more agitated.

She said, "I want to get out of here. This is terrible. I don't have to take this test. I don't have to do this. You can't make me. And besides, it is so noisy in here, I can barely think."

From my point of view, it was extremely quiet. Our

offices were on the quiet end of the hospital; it was like a morgue. Dead. Not much happening. People who did move around were so medicated that they didn't make too much noise. They just shuffled about quietly.

There we were, knee to knee, she, twitching and jerking and I, having to complete this Rorschach test so that it would be in her chart. I finally stopped the test and listened with her a moment.

I asked her what it sounded like. She said it sounded like a machine gun. Like somebody was killing somebody in the next room with a machine gun. So I listened. I said, "When you hear it, could you point it out?"

She said, "It's constant."

"OK, if it stops, would you tell me when it stops?"

So we sat together, listening. Just the two of us, listening. Test put aside; "she's the patient, I'm the psychologist" put aside because I was truly interested in finding out what was going on with this woman. I was no longer ready to dismiss her perceptions as auditory hallucinations. So we listened together.

She said, "There, it stopped. No, it started again."

Finally, I discovered, based on the rhythm of her stopping and starting, that the sound that was so intrusive in her consciousness was the secretary's typing, three offices down.

It took an enormous amount of effort for me to listen, to hear what she was hearing. When I finally discovered it and got in some rhythm with her, she was extremely pleased. No one had ever believed that the sounds she was hearing were real. People simply dismissed her, deciding that the sound she was hearing was a product of her own fantasy.

Since the early seventies, elaborate theories of schizophrenia have been developed regarding information-processing. One of the theories on certain kinds of schizophrenia is that the schizophrenic doesn't develop filtering mechanisms as "normal" individuals do. Nonschizophrenics are able to filter out irrelevant sound or memory. For example, you are able to read these words while filtering out the sounds around you, without even knowing it.

Each one of us has tones, firings, in our ears. There is a form of meditation where yogis listen to the sounds of their own vibrating eardrums. Yogis claim that if you focus on the sounds of your own vibrating eardrums, they become like trumpets, heaven's trumpets. With careful listening, time slows down. With the letting go of discriminating consciousness, sound becomes quite slow, wonderfully melodic.

But for some schizophrenics, this process requires very little meditation. Sound is so loud, and their ability to filter is so impaired, that they hear quite strongly what is normally filtered out.

I sat with this woman and listened and said, "That's the sound of the typewriter the secretary is typing on down the hall."

"Really? I don't believe you!"

"Yes, you don't believe me, but it does not have to be something bad."

"I still don't believe you."

"OK, but let us find out so you do not have to believe or not believe."

We walked down the hall slowly and we listened. Sure enough, she realized that it was simply the sound of the typewriter.

I don't know that it made any difference that she and I explored that sound. I never saw her again. That was the nature of my internship. People came, I spent a little time with them, and they went away. I never knew whether she was discharged or what happened. But we spent an afternoon listening and discovering each other. One human being stopped and listened with another.

The Zen school in which I teach is called Kwan Um. The school was founded by Zen Master Seung Sahn and is named after the Bodhisattva of Compassion, Kwan Se Um Bosal. *Kwan Um* means "perceive sound." Kwan Se Um Bosal is the bodhisattva who attained enlightenment when hearing the sounds of the world, listening. The story of her enlightenment is that she came to complete realization hearing the cries and sufferings of all beings. In iconography, she is often depicted riding a cloud and pouring the waters of compassion over the world.

A bodhisattva is any person or being whose life-direction is to help others. Kwan Se Um Bosal is the Korean name for the archetypal bodhisattva of compassion. In Sanskrit her name is Avalokitesvara; in China her name is Kwan Yin; and in Japan her name is Kanzeon or Kannon. In the West, this archetype is represented by Mary, the mother of Jesus. Mary also came to realization of the compassionate mind through listening. When the angels came and told her she was to bear the child of God, she said, "Be it done unto me according to thy will."

Can we take a moment and listen, without listening to something in order to get the meaning out of it? Not making a discrimination, just listening. When someone talks, listen and perceive what is said. Are these three actions, two actions, or one action?

When a gong is struck and the vibration is heard, or when the stick hits the floor (*whack!*), there is sound, particular sound and hearing, particular hearing. Without the hearing faculty, there can be nothing heard. Hearing and sound are one movement. Perception of sound (hearing) and sound depend on each other.

Listening depends on nothing.

The mistake of *identifying* with the content of listening (what is heard) is continuous. And thus, there is belief in a solid, stable self. But the stuff of listening, which is sound (things heard), arises, dwells, and falls away. It is impermanent. Just as these words that are being read are arising, dwelling, and falling away. Just as all sensation arises, dwells, and falls away. So to create a fixed self by identifying with the stuff of listening—or for that matter, with the stuff of seeing, smelling, tasting, touching, or thinking—is to make a most grievous error. And yet the tendency to identify with the impermanent continues, and suffering is unending.

Our minds are not separate in listening. Minds become separate when there is interpretation of what is heard, the content. She says, "Oh, he said that." And he says, "Oh, she said this." And she says, "Oh!" and he says, "Ah!" There is a falling into the erroneous habit of identifying with impermanent phenomena, with content, a mind of measurement, of comparison, of judgment, of mine, of yours, of this, of that, of illusions, of phantoms, of meanings.

Zen Master Hakuin lived in a small village. One of the villagers' daughters was betrothed to a wealthy man's son. She was in love with another boy and became pregnant by her lover. Afraid to shame her family, she told her father that the child was the son of the local Zen master. When the child was born, the father brought his grandson to the temple and said, "He is your baby; you take him."

Receiving the child, Hakuin said, "Is that so?" He went to town each day to beg milk for the child. The townspeople were abusive and judgmental but took pity on the child and gave milk.

The child's mother, longing for her baby, told her father the truth. Contrite, the father went back to the temple and humbly said, "My daughter has confessed that this child is not yours, that you are not the father." Giving the baby back, the Zen master simply said, "Is that so?"

Unlike Hakuin's simple listening and responding, most people listen through a particular template. It is as if one is taking a picture and there are many lenses over the camera. Colored lenses, distorting lenses, shading lenses, perhaps lenses that are focal, leaving out the peripheral, or peripheral, leaving out the focal. Years and years of conditioning habit have caused a buildup, a filtering system through which the world is experienced. When one listens, things heard are distorted by one's point of view, one's opinion. "This is not my baby." There is no clear hearing of what is being said. "Here is another mouth to feed." What is heard is one's *opinion* about what is said. Our particular version of what is being said is heard; listening takes on a version, legs painted on a snake.

But when particular forms are dropped and habits of hearing are let go, one can't help but listen. Listening is entered fully. Just listening in wonder, with no conditions or expectations. Open. The jet rumbling overhead. The whisper of cloth as people shift slightly on their cushions. The faint rustling of leaves outside. The *whoosh* of eyelashes. The parting of lips. The pulse in the fingertips. The imperceptible. The unheard. The sound of listening. It is only when we listen without opinion, condition, or situation that we know our correct function, moment by moment.

Someone gives you a newborn baby: find it some milk.

The fundamental ground of all existence, of all senses (eyes, ears, nose, tongue, body, and mind), has the same root—Emptiness, *shunyata*. In the eyes, listening is called seeing; in the nose, listening is called smelling; at the surface of the skin, listening is called touching; in the mind, listening is called thinking. In the heart, listening is called loving. And in the belly, listening is called knowing. Thus, listening and seeing, listening and hearing, listening and smelling, listening and tasting, listening and touching, listening and thinking, listening and loving, listening and knowing are all identical at the root, manifesting differently at the surface. Turning the hearing faculty inward to the source of listening, we realize the source of everything.

Listening and the Buddha's Teaching

Historically, bodhisattvas have attained enlightenment in different ways. Some have attained it through the faculty of hearing, some through the faculty of seeing, some through the sensation of water on their skin. But most direct is the practice of listening. With the hearing faculty turned inward, what is the sound of listening?

Ananda was heading for the gathering of buddhas and bodhisattvas and the disciples of the Buddha at Jetta Grove. The Buddha Shakyamuni was to offer there a discourse that would later be known as the Surangama Sutra. Ananda, who was the Buddha's cousin and constant attendant, was expected, for he had a perfect memory and could remember everything that the Buddha had ever said, right down to the smallest detail, the finest nuance. It was his job to record the discourses, thus giving us the sutras. But with all that he heard and remembered, he didn't attain enlightenment until well after the Buddha died.

It is said that as Ananda was heading for the gathering, he stopped to beg for food at the home of a courtesan who had a beautiful daughter named Pchiti. The mother, of course, knew that Ananda was a disciple of the Buddha; and since Ananda was practicing deeply in those days, he had a glow about him. The mother thought, "This monk would be a fine catch for my dear Pchiti." She put a spell on Ananda so that he would fall in love with Pchiti.

Ananda had already seen Pchiti through the window as he came to the house. He was struck by her grace and beauty and needed very little encouragement from the mother's spell to fall in love with her. When he met Pchiti face to face, he fell deeply in love. He was content to sit in her room and make love to her day and night. He felt he had found the deepest meaning in life and basked in her affections.

All this time, the Buddha was sitting with his other disciples, waiting, completely aware of Ananda's involvement with Pchiti. Now from one perspective, Ananda's detour can be seen as an error, a mistake. From a judging mind, we can see his detour as a falling by the wayside into the path of sexuality and sensuality, which would never lead him to enlightenment. Yet, although he didn't realize it at the time, Ananda was a great bodhisattva, and falling deeply and sincerely in love with Pchiti was an act of compassion that would eventually bring her in touch with the Buddha's teaching.

The Buddha, still waiting, sent Manjusri off to the place where Ananda was staying with Pchiti. "Ananda, come out! The Buddha is waiting for you." "Oh my," said Ananda as he awoke from his bliss-stupor. "And bring your friend with you." All three went to the meeting and were received by the Buddha.

Then the Lord Buddha struck his gong and asked Ananda if he had heard the sound of it.

Ananda replied that he had. After the vibration of the sound had died away, the Lord Buddha inquired:—Do you still hear? Ananda replied that he no longer heard it.

The Lord Buddha struck the gong again and asked:—Did you hear the striking of the gong? Ananda replied:—Yes, Blessed Lord.

Then the Lord Buddha said to Ananda:—Why do you reply at one time that you hear and at another time that you do not hear?

Ananda replied at once:—Blessed Lord, when the gong was struck I heard the sound, but when the vibrations died away the sound ceased. That is what I meant when I said at one time that I heard, and at another that I did not hear.

Again, the Lord Buddha struck the gong and inquired of Ananda if he could still hear. Ananda replied that he could. After a while when the sound had ceased, the Lord Buddha inquired again:—Do you still hear?

Ananda replied, a little impatiently:—No, Blessed Lord, the sound has ceased, how can I hear?

Then the Lord Buddha said:—Ananda, what is the meaning of it all? At one time you say you hear and at another time you say you do not hear?

Ananda replied:—Blessed Lord, when the gong is struck, there is a sound. After a time the sound ceases, then there is no sound.

The Lord Buddha interrupted, saying:—Ananda, why do you make such confused statements?

Ananda retorted:—Blessed One, why do you charge me with making confused statements, when I speak only of facts?

The Lord Buddha replied:—Ananda, why, indeed! When I asked whether you had heard the sound of the gong, you replied that you had heard it, but when I asked you if you could still hear, you replied at one time that you could, and at another time that you could not. You do not seem to realize that the sound of the gong, the hearing of the sound, and the perception of the hearing are three different things, for you replied without any recognition of the difference. That is why I said that you were making confused statements.

There is a difference between "sound" and "no sound," and "hearing" and "no hearing." Sound and no sound are momentary, while hearing and no hearing are permanent. Sound and no sound are imaginary, hearing belongs to the pure Essence of Mind. Ananda, you speak in error when you say there is no more hearing just because the sound ceases. If it is true that hearing ends with the cessation of noise, it would mean that the ear organ has been destroyed. When the gong was struck again, it would no longer have been heard, but you heard it so it means that you could hear all along. So you should recognize that your hearing of the sound and your not hearing of it are related to the existence or nonexistence of the sound, and not to the perception of the ear. If you remember this, your hearing nature will not seem to you to become at one time existent and at another time nonexistent.

Should the hearing nature really vanish, then by whom will the vanishing be realized? Therefore, Ananda, the sound object within the scope of the hearing nature has its own death and rebirth. It is not when you note the existence of the sound or the nonexistence of the sound that you should think that your hearing nature is in existence or not in existence.

As your mind is still in a topsy-turvy condition when it mistakes the sound to be the same as your hearing nature, it is no wonder that your mind is bewildered in the entanglements caused by mistaking the nature of permanency as being the same as destructibility. Therefore, it is not right for you to say that as soon as hearing is separated from such conditions as motion and motionlessness, impassibility or passibility, that the perception of hearing has no essential nature of its own. The hearing faculty can be likened to a sleepy fellow of this world, sleeping soundly on his bed. During his sleep, some of his family are batting their clothes as they wash them, and some were hulling rice by pounding it, and the sound of the batting and the pounding mingle with his dreams and are but the rat-a-pan and the dum-dum of a drum. In his dream he wondered why the ding-dong should sometimes sound like coming from wood and sometimes like coming from stone. When he awoke, he immediately realized that the sound came from batting clothes on wood and pounding rice on stone. He told his family about his dream and how bewildered he was by such sounds coming from a drum.

Ananda! In his dream the man did not think of conceptions of motion and motionlessness in relation to the sounds, or the passibility and impassability in relation to the organ of hearing, but though his body was asleep, yet the essential part of hearing was as clear as ever. By means of this illustration, you must see that in spite of the destruction of your body and the gradual exhaustion of the vitality of your life, that the essential nature of the hearing-conception is not destroyed nor caused to vanish.

Therefore, as all sentient beings from beginningless time have always hankered after beautiful sights and musical sounds, filling their thinking minds with thought after thought and causing it to be always active, and never realizing that by nature it was pure, mysterious, permanent and Essential, thus causing them, instead of following the path of permanency, to follow the current of transitory deaths and rebirths. Consequently, there has been life after life ever recurring and ever filled with contaminations, impermanency and suffering.*

---

*Goddard, Dwight, ed., *A Buddhist Bible* (Boston: Beacon Press, 1970), pp. 210–12.

At the very first striking of the gong, Pchiti entered fully into the sound of the gong, attained the deepest and most profound enlightenment, and took her place among the great bodhisattvas.

If we have an idea about what it means to be a monk, Ananda's love for Pchiti may be seen as a mistake in spiritual direction. But because the part cannot know the whole, we cannot predict what relationships will lead to realization. Once there was a thief who saw the monk Joju walking on a path. He followed him to his hotel with the intention of robbing him. The thief waited until late at night and opened the door to Joju's room. When the thief opened the door, he opened onto a garden with a cypress tree in it. Thinking he made a mistake, he opened the next door down. There, he saw the same garden with a beautiful cypress tree in the middle. As the thief was about to shut the door, Joju came out of his samadhi. At that time, Joju was practicing with the kong-an "The Cypress Tree in the Garden," and his concentration was so deep and pure that he would actually manifest as the kong-an during his meditation. Impressed by Joju's ability to transform himself, the thief asked if he could teach him how to do this. He thought of how much he could steal if he could transform himself so people could not recognize him. He practiced very hard to master this art of transformation, became enlightened, and then became a great Zen master. He never stole again but only helped all people.

What Shakyamuni Buddha teaches in this part of the Surangama Sutra is that although sound appears, and we hear particular sounds as they arise, dwell, and fall away, we are not those sounds. We are not what arises, dwells, and falls away. We are not what is heard. The sound-object has its own death and rebirth. The mind is bewildered in entanglements caused by mistaking the impermanent for the permanent. Sound is transient, but listening is unborn, uncreated, unconditioned, and eternal, our true nature. We are listening: listening itself. And so it is with all the stuff of life. Our bodies, our minds, all phenomena, change and continue the round of death and rebirth, of arising and passing away. But we, our fundamental nature, our listening, do not change.

We benefit by this discourse. We benefit by the confused statements of Ananda and his error of confusing his listening nature with things heard.

Ananda's gift is the transcription of this sutra, the transmission of these words down to us. Ananda's gift was also to fall in love and to bring Pchiti to the discourse, where she could hear and—beyond all hearing— realize her true nature, her listening mind, and attain complete awakening. Yet it is said that Ananda did not attain enlightenment until well after the Buddha was dead but remained, as he was in the Surangama Sutra, unclear about the nature of things heard.

Well after the Buddha was dead, and when there were no more of the Buddha's sutras to remember and record, Ananda became the student of Mahakasyapa. Mahakasyapa, the first Zen patriarch, received, as a sign of his direct mind-to-mind transmission of the Dharma, the Buddha's robes and bowls.

One morning, Ananda and Mahakasyapa were having an exchange near the flagpole on which one of the monks was raising a flag to signal that a Dharma talk was to be given. Ananda asked Mahakasyapa, "Did the Buddha transmit anything to you other than his robe and bowl?"

Mahakasyapa answered, "Ananda!"

And Ananda said, "Yes."

"Knock down the flagpole at the front gate of the monastery!"

It is complete; we have everything we need. "Ananda!" "Yes!" "Knock down the flagpole, the Dharma talk is over!" Let go of words, let go of things heard. "Knock down the flagpole." Talking about the Dharma is over. "Ananda, knock down the flagpole!" No more fingers pointing to the moon, only the moon itself. Direct transmission, generous, without any kind of holding. And Ananda gained deep realization, listened beyond all things heard, and awakened. Calling and answering is all there is. There is no secret beyond the immediacy of this.

Listening as Bowing

In Zen practice there are four primary formal practices. In fact, we have ten thousand practices, a myriad of practices: the practice of listening to a friend, the practice of listening to the morning birds, the practice of feeling the cushion and floor supporting us, the practice of thinking and considering and speculating about the future, the practice of brushing our teeth, the practice of going to the toilet. But because we have thinking, we can divide our practices into the formal and informal. We use our formal practices as encouragement for mindfulness, to help in our listening, and to help us become aware in this moment, to come fully to this moment.

The four primary formal practices are bowing practice, sitting and walking practice, chanting practice, and formal-meal practice. Bowing practice is a practice that is a part of all religious practice. Hands together in prayer, the head or body bowed.

With our hands in prayer position, there are three types of bow. There is sitting-bow, where we bend at the waist and make our body parallel to the floor, almost touching the forehead to the floor. There is standing-bow, where we put our hands in prayer position and bend at the waist ninety degrees, almost parallel with the floor, letting the prayer hands fall until almost touching the knees.

And third, there is the prostration-bow (great bow), where we start with the standing-bow and then fall to our knees. We bend down, touch the mat with our forehead, turn our palms upward, and cross our feet so that the top of the left foot covers the sole of the right foot. Then we come back into a kneeling position, then stand again. This is one complete bow. In the Kwan Um School of Zen, we make 108 prostration (great) bows each morning before we chant and sit.

There is a famous monk, from the Tang dynasty in China, named Seon Do Sunim. Seon Do Sunim always bowed to everything. Whatever he met, he bowed to it. He bowed to cows, he bowed to dogs, he bowed to insects, he bowed to horses, he bowed to women, he bowed to men, he bowed to laymen, he bowed to monks, he bowed to chairs. He bowed to everything because "everything is Buddha." He bowed to Buddha as Buddha appeared again and again in the myriad forms. The practice of bowing to everything one meets means no thinking or evaluating, only bowing.

Bowing is a powerful way to see into the error of self-centered activity. In bowing, self-centered activity slowly, slowly diminishes and the Buddha-mind manifests like a lotus blossom, blooming and shining forth. When the Buddha-mind is manifest, there is no distinction. All things appear and disappear as they are, a manifestation of Buddha. When we bow with this mind, we bow to our true self.

Bowing is a clear and direct way to see karma. If we want to wake up to the habitual ways by which we deal with daily life, there must be a willingness to bow. Imagine all that we are reluctant to bow to: the clerk who gives us a hard time exchanging a purchase; a friend who has betrayed our confidence; all those with political, religious, and personal views that are not consistent with our own; those who have committed heinous crimes.

At first, bowing may seem to be worshipping an image. There is a dualistic quality. I am bowing to that. We bow to our teacher in the morning; we bow to each other when we meet on the path. In the beginning, bowing seems to be deferring to something else. Yet if we really pay keen attention during the process of bowing, we will see that bowing is not separate from breath. When we fall to our knees with our head to the mat, we see that bowing is no different than exhalation. And the rising from the mat and putting our hands back in prayer position is no different from inhalation. And so with bowing, we are bowing with our whole body-mind. We are listening. Our listening is with body and mind together. As we bow, we listen fully with the whole body and mind, spinal column, knees, thighs, feet, hands, forehead to the mat, listening completely, standing up, rising, in a full body breath.

Bowing, we are bowing in the unborn, undifferentiated mind. Bowing is not to attain something or to express deference. Bowing is as straightforward as breath itself, rising and falling, rising and falling like the ocean tides; like the movement of the sun and the moon; like dolphins as they swim along, surfacing for air and diving back into the water. Bowing is the expression of the universality of existence in its ebbing and flowing, in its yin and yang, in its yes and no, in its up and down, in its masculinity and femininity, in its mother and father reconciled as one. Bowing is the complete expression of opposites. So in our bowing, falling and rising, opposites are transcended and reconciled, and there is only bowing.

There was a famous monk from China (and there are still monks in California), whose practice was to bow as a way of moving from one point to another. Chinese monks have gone from central China to the birthplace of the Buddha, bowing the whole way, taking three steps and making a prostration-bow, taking three more steps, then another prostration-bow, moving across an entire country. Imagine going from your door to the mailbox this way, let alone across an entire country! The mind that is in a hurry to get from here to there is confronted immediately. The notion of becoming something or obtaining something gets frustrated quite quickly in this kind of practice.

When I first met Zen Master Seung Sahn, I was running eight miles a day and had all the marvelous benefits from running that much. A friend would come every morning, and we would go out and run in the fields, meeting the morning sun. On the weekends, sometimes we would run twenty miles—drive out to the country, run ten miles away from the car, and then run ten miles back. On one run, I twisted my knee and couldn't run anymore. Zen Master Seung Sahn said, "Why don't you try bowing? I used to run for my heart, but now I do a thousand bows every day. This is not only good for your body but it helps all beings." So I began bowing one thousand times every day instead of running. It is said that Chinese Zen Master Ma Jo bowed so many times that he had calluses on his forehead.

Bowing is a wide practice. Not only is there clear spiritual expression in bowing, but there is all the aerobic benefit of running, and it is low-impact. What is best about bowing as a spiritual practice is that no matter what the state of your mind, you can bow. If you are confused and distraught, you can still put your forehead to the mat. If you are in enormous doubt and have no faith in any practice at all—or when you are sitting quietly, your mind is so chaotic you can hardly bear it—you can still put your forehead to the mat.

Whether you bow a thousand times a day or only

three times each day, you can let your small self go. Holding nothing in the bow, putting the forehead to the mat, letting go of all fixed ideas of self in the falling and rising—it doesn't matter what state of mind you are in. It doesn't matter what condition your life is in or what chaotic feeling has arisen in you—there is only bowing. By putting yourself fully into bowing, all karma lifts and you are present in the moment. The mind of desire, the mind of longing, the mind of clinging, the mind of impermanence, the mind of disappointment all dissolve in the bowing moment.

Try bowing to whatever you meet. Whether you formally bow and put your head to the ground or simply bow from the waist (or bow in the mind), try bowing to everything as a way of listening. Bow to the trees, bow to the sounds of the birds, bow to a friend's voice on a summer morning. Bowing means putting aside *I, me, mine,* letting go of all self-centered activity. In bowing, we cut through dualistic thinking. Just bowing.

Two monks came to visit Zen Master Joju. They traveled over a thousand miles to see him. They came to the gate, and Joju came out of his hut to meet them. They greeted him, "Oh, great Zen Master Joju, we have come a thousand miles to see you." Joju lowered his head, turned, and went back into the hut. What is the meaning of Joju's bow?

Listening as Mantra Practice

There is a listening practice that some spiritual disciplines call mantra practice. A mantra is a word or a phrase repeated and listened to with the whole body-mind. There are many mantras to choose from. It does not matter which one you choose. A couple of often-used mantras are the Hail Mary and the Our Father. I have heard of people using childhood prayers and songs, Native American chants, favorite hymns. Most important is that the mantra does not have so much meaning and association that it loses its simplicity and immediacy. There are a multitude of mantras, with a multitude of meanings, but they all point to the same thing: the mind of not-becoming.

Zen Master Seung Sahn says that if you can say "Coca-Cola," and if there is a complete giving of yourself to it, then it will work as well as something more sacred by reputation. The most important thing is just doing the mantra. In mantra practice, do not go left, do not go right. Do not go ahead of the mantra. And do not lag behind the mantra. Only do the mantra, letting go of everything else, entering the mantra completely.

Mantra practice is difficult because it is susceptible to ambition. Mantra can mistakenly be used to try to bring something about, to cause something to happen, or to otherwise align with ego-intention. There can be a tendency to use mantra to attain some ideal state of mind in the future rather than to express true self moment by moment. In entering the mantra, to express true self, all must be given to it without hope of attaining anything.

In mantra practice, you listen to the voice of the eternal, the voice before your mother was born. Each mantra is the sound that contains all sound. Every mantra is the sound of embracing the entire world, the entire Universe, the particular and the absolute. In mantra practice, the mind becomes one-pointed. Keeping this one point, the mind becomes clear. When the mind is clear, compassionate action is primary.

The following are a few common mantras in Buddhist and Christian practices:

Gate (pronounced gah-tay), *gate, paragate, parasamgate, bodhi svaha* Meanings: Beyond, beyond, beyond the great beyond, alleluia. Or, put it all down.

Ji Jang Bosal Meaning: Bodhisattva of children, and those dying or dead.

Kwan Se Um Bosal Meaning: Bodhisattva of Compassion

Namu Amitabul Meaning: Become one with the Buddha of the Pure Land, or the Pure Light Buddha of infinite time, infinite space.

Namu chilguji bul modae junje bosal Meaning: Become one with the mother of all buddhas, purveyor of healing and compassion.

Om nam Meaning: Original Purity

Om mani padme hum Meaning: The jewel is in the lotus. (Opposites, e.g., masculine and feminine, become one.)

Lord Jesus Christ, Son of God, have mercy on me. Or Lord Jesus Christ Meaning: (This is called the Jesus prayer.)

Yahweh Meaning: Old Testament name of God

Ohm Meaning: Universal sound

Once there was a young girl named Sul who had the good fortune to grow up in China in the town where great Zen Master Ma Jo lived. She would visit Ma Jo with her father whenever he went to the temple. Ma Jo liked Sul very much and could see that she would be a great teacher someday. One day, Sul and her father were visiting Ma Jo, who said to Sul, "You have been visiting me here for many years, and every time you come you bring me a present. Sometimes you bring fruit, sometimes you bring cake. But in all this time I have never given you a present. Today, I have a very special present for you. It is a present that will make up for all the presents I did not give you in the past. Please accept this present and treasure it with your whole life. The present I have for you is the name of the Bodhisattva of Compassion, *Kwan Se Um Bosal.* Always keep her name with you, saying it over and over."

Sul's eyes lit up. She knew what a special gift this was, as she had heard all about Kwan Se Um Bosal from her father. She thanked Ma Jo with a deep bow, and from that day on she kept the name Kwan Se Um Bosal in her *tandien* and on her tongue. Whatever she was doing and wherever she went, she listened to her inner voice singing "Kwan Se Um Bosal." When she would go for water, she sang "Kwan Se Um Bosal" at the top of her lungs, and when she lay in her bed at night, falling asleep, she kept the mantra going silently so as not to disturb her family.

After several years, she gained the reputation of being odd. Other children stopped playing with her, and their parents felt sorry for her parents. This did not bother Sul at all. She chanted the mantra *Kwan Se Um Bosal* or kept it silently inside all day and all night. One day she was washing clothes at the stream. She was beating the clothing with a stick to get the dirt out when she heard the sound of Ma Jo's temple bell in the distance. All of a sudden, the sound of the stick and the sound of the bell merged. Her mind burst open, and she was filled with great bliss. The whole world was a manifestation of *Kwan Se Um Bosal*. The sound of the stream, the children laughing in the distance, and the sound of the temple bell were all Kwan Se Um Bosal's voice. The sky, the hills, and the trees were Kwan Se Um Bosal's body. She was none other than Kwan Se Um Bosal; and her father, mother, Zen Master Ma Jo, the neighborhood children, and everyone she met were all manifestations of *Kwan Se Um Bosal*. After this experience, she never chanted *Kwan Se Um Bosal* again.

Over the next few days, her parents became even more worried about her. She seemed different than she had been. Her father would peek in on her meditating in her room. One day, he saw her sitting on a copy of the Lotus Sutra. Buddhist altars in those days always had a copy of the Lotus Sutra on them. Sul's father was furious. He broke into the room and demanded, "What are you doing? This is a holy scripture. Have you no respect?!"

Sul was not upset. She simply smiled and said, "The truth is not contained in words."

These words struck her father's mind. "Then where is truth?" he asked.

"If I told you, you would not believe me," said Sul. "Go ask Zen Master Ma Jo."

Sul's father went to the temple and told Ma Jo the

story. Frustrated and worried, the father asked, "Has Sul gone crazy?"

"No, no, you are very lucky. Your daughter has not gone crazy. It is you who are crazy in this," said Ma Jo.

Ma Jo then made a large calligraphy to give to Sul:

When you hear the wooden chicken crow in the evening,
You will know the country where your mind was born.
Outside my house, in the garden,
The willow is green, the flower is red.

"Please put this up in your daughter's room."

When Sul came home from school and saw the poem, she said, "Oh, Zen Master Ma Jo is also just like this." She returned the sutra to the altar and lit a stick of incense, watching the smoke rise in an endless stream as she sat listening.

Sul continued to practice listening, day and night. Sometimes she would sit quietly in front of her altar. At night, she would lie in her bed and listen to the rain or the frogs or the night animals. Other times, she would simply listen as she went about her daily routine. Her listening practice never stopped, no matter what she was doing. One day, she was visiting Zen Master Ma Jo when a friend of his, Zen Master Ho Am, was also visiting.

Ho Am looked at Sul and said, "I hear that this young girl has had some big experience. I will test your mind. In the sutra, it says, 'The great Mount Sumeru fits into a mustard seed; someone enters, and the mountain breaks into ten thousand pieces.' What does this mean?"

Sul threw her teacup against the wall, breaking it into hundreds of pieces.

Ma Jo enjoyed this response but said, "Now I will test you. We often use the word *karma* in Buddhism. What does this word mean?"

Sul asked, "Please ask me the question once more."

Ma Jo said, "In all of the Buddha's teaching, he depends on the concept of karma. What is the meaning of karma?"

Sul bowed and said, "Thank you very much."

Ma Jo smiled and bowed back. They quietly looked at each other, beaming.

Sul grew up to be a great Zen master. She never was ordained but married and raised a large family. Her life seemed ordinary, but in this ordinary life she was clear and profound. Many people came to her for help and teaching.

When Sul was very old, one of her granddaughters died unexpectedly. At the funeral, Sul cried and cried without holding back. People were polite for a while, but soon they became uncomfortable. Finally, one man came up to Sul and demanded, "You are a great Zen master. You are supposed to understand that there is no life and no death, yet you make a fool of yourself crying at this funeral. How do you expect people to believe in you? Why has the death of your granddaughter caused a problem for you?"

Sul immediately stopped crying and looked the man in the eye. "My tears are tears for all beings. When

I cry, my granddaughter and all transient beings hear these cries. By listening to my crying, they enter nirvana. Crying is better than all the sutras. Do you understand?"

With deep humility, the man bowed and said, "Thank you for your teaching."

Sul looked out at the guests who were all quietly listening, smiled, and said, "Thank you all for coming."

Questions that appear from this story are "What is the meaning of Sul's tears, and how are they different from the others' tears? How does Sul's crying help her granddaughter and other transient beings? If you open your mouth to explain, you miss the essence. If you don't answer, you evade the truth. What can you do?"

We may practice with *Om mani padme hum* or with *Kwan Se Um Bosal, Kwan Se Um Bosal*. But we practice always in the context of the Great Question: Who is saying the mantra?

Om mani padme hum.

Listening as Chanting

A fundamental aspect of chanting is listening. Without listening while chanting, there is no harmony. Most spiritual practices have chanting as part of their service. Tibetan monks chant in their low multichord tones. Christian monks chant Gregorian chants in Latin. Sufi dervishes and Native Americans also use chanting as a spiritual practice.

When one chants with a group, there are three voices. One voice is from our mouth. A second voice is from another's mouth. The third voice is the common voice, the group voice, the voice that expresses the harmony of the sangha, or community. Our particular voice is also a result of harmony, the harmony of our body-*sangha,* which includes the tongue, lungs, heart, and mind. Each of these can also be broken down into its particular sanghas, and broken down again and again, infinitely. Chanting is the expression of the harmony of community within community, sangha within sangha.

Zen Master Seung Sahn attained enlightenment chanting the Great Dharani (Appendix 1) on a solo retreat. Ten days after being ordained as a Zen Buddhist monk, Haeng Won (Seung Sahn's monk name, which means "complete action") climbed Won Gak Mountain (the Mountain of Perfect Enlightenment) to begin a hundred-day chanting retreat. He was twenty-one years old.

For one hundred days, Haeng Won chanted the Great Dharani, twenty hours a day. All he ate was a simple diet of dried pine needles crushed into a powder. By the fiftieth day, his body exhausted, Haeng Won was assailed with doubt. He wanted to go home. Packing his knapsack, the young monk felt that he couldn't stay but that he also couldn't leave. So he unpacked his belongings. Several times during the remainder of the retreat, Haeng Won packed and unpacked, but he never left.

Haeng Won had many fantastic experiences during his retreat. Everything appeared. Demons appeared. Tigers, dragons, and huge beetles appeared. Buddha and Kwan Se Um Bosal also appeared. During the last week, two young boys with angelic faces appeared and accompanied Haeng Won during walking meditation. Walking down the mountain path, Haeng Won walked between two huge boulders. His young companions, one on each side of him, walked right through the boulders. At the end of the week, the two young boys disappeared.

On the hundredth day, Haeng Won had an opening. While chanting the Great Dharani, his body and mind fell away and he experienced infinite time, infinite space. He realized that the sound of his voice and the sound of the stream were one; that the trees and rocks were none other than his true self; and that everything he saw, smelled, tasted, touched, and heard was the truth. He realized that the truth is just like this.

The next morning, Haeng Won saw a man walking up the mountain road and heard some crows flying out of a tree. He composed the following poem:

The road at the bottom of Won Gak Mountain
is not the present road.
The man climbing with his backpack
is not a man of the past.
Tok, tok, tok—his footsteps
transfix past and present.
Crows out of a tree.
Caw, caw, caw!!

Soon after coming down off Won Gak Mountain, Haeng Won met with his teacher, Zen Master Ko Bong, and was given Dharma transmission and the name Seung Sahn, which is a famous mountain in China.

Zen Master Seung Sahn offers the following comment on chanting as a practice:

> *Chanting meditation means keeping a not-moving mind and perceiving the sound of your own voice. Perceiving your voice means perceiving your True Self or true nature. Then you and the sound are not separate, which means that you and the whole universe are not separate. Thus, to perceive our true nature is to perceive universal substance.*
>
> *At first, people come to chanting practice with strong opinions, strong likes and dislikes. For many people, chanting practice is not so easy; much confused thinking, many likes and dislikes appear. But doing chanting practice correctly, perceiving the sound of your own voice and the voices all around you, your mind becomes clear. In clear mind there is no like or dislike, only the sound.*
>
> *Perceiving sound means everything is universal sound: birds singing, thunder crashing, dogs barking. If your mind is clear, everything is perceived as it is. When the mind is clear like space, everything is clear. Red comes; red. White comes; white. Someone is happy: I am happy. Someone is sad: I am sad. Someone is hungry: give them food. The name for this is Great Love, Great Compassion, the Great Bodhisattva Way.*
>
> *Sound in Zen practice is very simple. Any sound will do. What's important is to perceive the sound and become one with it, without separation, without making "I" and "sound." At the moment of*

true perceiving, there is no thought, no separation, only perceiving sound.

So during chanting, perceive your own voice and the voice of others. Just perceive the sound of the bell or the sound of the moktak. Cut off all thinking. Then your wisdom-mind will grow, you will get enlightenment and save all beings from suffering. *

The meaning of one's life is created from one's own personal history. But in the center of sound, there is no meaning at all. All sounds are the sound of Buddha's voice, and they return to the original meaning. This is the practice of chanting: all sounds returning to the primary meaning.

One does not have to understand a chant to fully express its deepest aspect. One may have no idea what a chant means until the translation is read, and even then the meaning often cannot be remembered. One can read all the translations of the chants several times, but in true chanting the meaning does not appear. When you are chanting, it is just the sound, shared together. All intellectual meaning is dropped. Once you have realized the primary meaning of all sound, then what is the function of sound? All sound has correct function. "Correct" doesn't imply some moral issue. It only means that if someone is crying for food, feed him. If someone is crying for shelter, give him a place to stay. If someone is crying because he is not getting enough attention, hit

*Zen Master Seung Sahn, *Perceive World Sound* (Providence: Primary Point Press, undated), introduction.

him on the head. The correct function of our listening is compassion.

We chant each morning in our Zen community. In the Morning Bell Chant (Appendix 2), we chant the following seven times (later, five times):

Na-mu A-mi-ta-bul

Namu Amitabul means "become one with Namu Amitabul, Buddha of the Pure Land, Buddha of infinite time and infinite space." To become one means not to be separate from infinite time, infinite space, even for one millisecond. To realize the timelessness and the space-lessness of all things. To realize not-becoming.

For the rest of my life, I vow to have no distracting thought, to follow only Amitabul, the Buddha of infinite time and infinite space, a pure filament of radiant light that permanently joins every mind state, moment to moment. Never straying from this golden form. Holding a bead *mala*, the Dharma world is perceived. With emptiness as the string, there is nothing unconnected. All is complete and as it is, contained in the listening mind.

It does not take any complicated philosophical understanding to realize this. One can experience this in the chant itself. *Namu Amitabul.* Magically dissolving all thought, all separation, even for the worst chanter. Even when stumbling over all other parts, the difficult tones, the shifting of melodies that are characteristic of this chant, all difficulty with chanting, all liking and disliking, vanish. Dwelling in the mind-equalizing manifestation of universal energy, a marvelous, clear awareness appears, and all suffering that arises from the dualistic mind falls away.

When the mind is pure and clear, all speech is pure and clear, like the bright sound of a bell. Everything said, every word, every syllable, is a hell-shattering sound that brings all sentient beings' suffering to an end. Every sound uttered is the name Amitabul, is the name Kwan Se Um Bosal. The voice becomes a raft for all beings to realize their original nature, to realize universal substance and energy, which is compassion and wisdom, our birthright. Our effort in chanting, and in mantra practice as well, is to realize the mind of not-becoming. In expressing our original nature, we express the original nature of all beings, and this very expression is salvation from suffering.

Listening as Sitting Meditation

Ideally, we should need no special practices. Our nature is already Buddha-nature. But because there is thinking and its resultant karma, we practice meditation. We practice sitting quietly, letting thoughts settle like dust on a dirt road after a car goes by.

Before sitting, prepare a space in a quiet place, free from avoidable interruptions. You may want to make an altar as a focal point. In Korean Buddhism, the altar in the meditation hall typically has the four universal elements (earth, wind, water, and fire) represented. Earth is represented by a bowl of rice; wind is represented by incense; candles are lit representing fire. A water bowl is refreshed daily. Most Buddhist altars also have a sitting

Buddha, which represents the Absolute. When a friend or relative dies, that person's name is often put on the altar for a period of time. The spirit of the altar is to encourage awareness. Students sometimes find it helpful to put the picture of a friend, or person they are having a problem with, on their altar. The act of placing something on the altar is not a superstitious act to magically bring about a desired result but a practice of seeing everything as it is.

When you're sitting, it is important to be grounded. It is good to have three points of contact supporting your body. If you are sitting in a chair, have your feet flat on the floor. If you sit cross-legged, sit so that your knees touch the mat beneath you. Most important, keep your spine straight. Tip your pelvis forward so that your spine arches slightly at the small of your back. Lift your head from the crown. Relax your shoulders and slightly tuck your chin, lifting at the sternum. Place your hands in your lap, palms up, with the left hand over the right palm. Touch thumbs so that they make a bridge, never a mountain, never a valley. Slightly flare the arms, as if there were an egg in each armpit. Place the tongue at the roof of your mouth, with the tip of the tongue at the back of the top front teeth.

If you are new to sitting, this posture may be awkward at first. In time, it will become natural and relaxed. The state of the mind is revealed in the posture of the body. Old body-habits return while we sit, so the practice of sitting can help us return to our best posture. Listen to your body. By your listening, the body will ease into a position or a harmony of its own. Returning to a bright, open pose, we return to the moment.

While sitting, listen to your breath. Listen, and the breath roars like the ocean. Breathing in, we are born. Breathing out, we die. Our first breath is an inhalation without exception; and with this inhalation, everyone is born. With the exhalation, everyone dies. So our breath is very important. Our life is an unbroken chain of inhalations and exhalations. Listening to the breath is listening to our own life, the sound of our existence.

Our natural way to breathe is to distend the belly when inhaling and to let it collapse when exhaling. Sit quietly with awareness in the belly, allowing exhalation to give way to inhalation. The breath will return to its original nature, filling the whole body like a bellows when breathing in, and collapsing when breathing out. Newborn babies breathe naturally with expansion of the lower abdomen during the in-breath, and on the out-breath, the lower abdomen naturally collapses. It is not until our thinking habits appear that the breath pattern changes. Breath awareness returns us to our original breathing nature. Without breathing, there can be no listening realized. When we are holding our breath, listening is not manifest in awareness.

Two inches below the navel is the body's physiological center, often called the *hara,* the *tandien,* or energy garden. It is where we digest food. It is where we gestate in our mother's womb. When we are thinking, we lose energy out the top of our head. Sounds appear and thought follows them. When we practice hard, energy gathers, the center becomes stronger, and thought does not control the mind. When thought does not control the mind, the mind is clear and bright. When the mind is clear and bright, everything is clear and as it is. It is only when everything is perceived clearly that compassionate action is possible. We can listen from the tandien by waiting at the bottom of the exhalation. Without adjusting the breath in any particular way, simply wait at the end of the exhalation and allow the inhalation to come on its own.

Practice waiting at the end of the exhalation as one would wait for a long-distance call from a friend overseas. We know approximately when the friend is going to call but we do not know exactly. We turn off all other noise. Shut off the TV and radio. If someone is visiting, we excuse ourselves. We want to be ready. We don't want to miss the call. And we wait. Because this is our best friend, she always calls, sometimes a little early, sometimes a little later. But we wait and we are there, present for the call, listening and ready. Waiting for the inhalation as you would wait for the call of a friend, alert and mindful, putting aside all other distraction. In the discipline of waiting and being present to the breath, our center becomes strong.

When the center is strong and the mind is pure and clear, our original energy connects with Universal Energy. Some names for this are God-consciousness, Christ-consciousness, Buddha-mind or compassion—different names all pointing to the same phenomenon.

In the stillness of pure listening, original mind manifests and is not separate from Universal Mind. Distinctions typically given to sensation and phenomena are no longer dominant. Sensation is no longer fragmented, and senses are fully integrated. Mind is alert, awake, and able to perceive things as they are. In this clear perception, compassion flows.

Practicing *Mu* as Listening

The first kong-an in the *Mumonkan*, a famous collection
of kong-ans, is Mu. A monk asked Zen Master Joju,
"Does a dog have Buddha-nature?" Joju said, "MU!"
This is often the first kong-an assigned to new students
in Zen. The student is instructed to "take up Mu." Or
the student is asked the question "What is Mu?" Students are then instructed to keep Mu in their tandien
and concentrate all energy and attention on Mu, day
and night. With all your energy, take up Mu. Never separate from Mu. Become one with Mu!

When I began to practice Zen, I had a deep infatuation with Mu. I had read about Mu and had read
promises of enlightenment from its practice. For ten
years, I searched for a teacher who would assign me Mu.
For one reason or another, I was never assigned Mu in
the interview room. All this time I was practicing with
Mu, but there was an uncomfortable feeling. I felt like
an interloper because it was not assigned formally by a
Zen master. When I met Zen Master Seung Sahn, I asked
him to assign me Mu and he said, "Mu is not important.
What are you doing just now? That is the point." I let go
of Mu on his instruction and never talked about it again.
After a few years, my interest in "using" Mu returned,
and I began putting it in the tandien and letting it be the
focus of my attention. I was using Mu to follow the out-
breath, sometimes in a single long Mu, sometimes with
what is called bamboo Mu, in segments.

I had never mentioned to Zen Master Seung Sahn
that I was working with Mu again. One day, while driving to a retreat at Gethsemani Abbey with Zen Master

Seung Sahn, we were stopped at a traffic light. We had been silent for most of the trip, and I was listening to Mu in my tandien, quietly. Zen Master Seung Sahn turned to me and said, "Mu practice is not correct!" I was astonished. I just stared at him. My mind was confused. *How did he know I was practicing Mu? Why do some teachers like Mu and my teacher doesn't?* In a split second many questions flashed in my mind until finally only one remained: *What is this?* Zen Master Seung Sahn turned forward, pointed to the traffic signal, and said, "Green light: go." The mind relaxed, the car slowly moved forward, and we were driving down the road, blue sky above, black pavement below.

Any practice or teaching is only an expediency to arouse the not-knowing mind. All practices and teachings can obscure the truth. Particular practices like Mu, mantra, kong-an, chanting, or just sitting are fingers pointing to the moon. They point us in the direction but are not the moon itself. It is easy to form an attachment to a practice. Attaining the not-knowing mind of Joju just before he said "Mu!" is most important. In not-knowing, all practices then point the way to compassion.

There is a story about a monk who came to the temple to learn the Buddha-dharma. He was very confused and not very intelligent. His name was Sok Du, which translates roughly as "rock head." He tried very hard to study the sutras but was unable to understand them. Frustrated, he decided to try Zen practice. But he was so confused, he could not sit or chant. Whenever the Zen master gave a talk, Sok Du would eagerly sit in the front row but was unable to understand anything. He would leave the Dharma hall more confused than when he went in. So the master told him to do only work practice and assigned him to the kitchen. He worked very hard and helped the kitchen master. He was allowed only to be a helper because everything he did on his own, he would mess up.

One day he went to the master and said, "I don't understand Zen. Please teach me." The master said, "Please ask me a question." So Sok Du asked, "What is Buddha?" The Master said, "*Juk shim shi bul.*" This means "Buddha is mind." The monk misunderstood him and thought he said, "*Jip shin shi bul.*" This means "Buddha is grass shoes."

"Oh, thank you," he said. "This is a wonderful kong-an. Very difficult." And he left. When he was away from the master's presence, he became even more confused. "Buddha is grass shoes, Buddha is grass shoes. What does this mean?" All day and all night, his mind was absorbed in this question. What is the meaning of this? He kept this question for three years. He never went for another interview, never went to formal practice, and never asked the teacher about his kong-an. He worked all day in the kitchen and in the garden and was completely absorbed in the question "What is the meaning of 'Buddha is grass shoes'?"

One day, he was carrying water down the hill and fell. Everything flew up in the air, and the grass shoes he was wearing hit him on the head, broke, and fell to the ground.

His mind burst open and he ran to the Zen master. "I now understand! I now understand Buddha!"

"So what is Buddha?" asked the Zen master.

Sok Du took off one of his shoes and hit the master on the head.

"Only this?" asked the master.

"My shoes are broken," Sok Du replied.

Student and teacher burst into laughter and embraced.

When the not-knowing mind is clear and bright, whatever you see, hear, smell, taste, touch, or think—just like this—is the truth.

Chapter Two

Kong-Ans

Introduction to Kong-An Practice

ong-an means "public case." Kong-ans, or *koans,* are stories or situations that reveal the enlightened mind. A kong-an cannot be resolved by conventional linear thinking. For example, a popular kong-an is "The sound of one hand clapping." While we know the sound of two hands clapping, the sound of one hand does not make "sense." How can one hand by itself make sound? But because we are curious, and because the Way-seeking mind has an intelligence of its own, we look into it. Because we are going to die, these questions appear. Because we are going to die, everything appears. So we look into the question further. What is the sound of one hand clapping?

At first, it seems to be a curious intellectual puzzle. Looking further, there is the realization that the conventional, linear, self-centered way of seeing the human condition is perhaps a mistake because of its limitations. Looking further still, there is the realization that this question confronts the very issue of life and death.

It is like hanging from a tree by your teeth, with your arms and legs bound. A warrior comes by and asks you, "Why did Bodhidharma come West?" If you open your mouth, you will fall to your death. If you don't answer, the warrior who asked the question will be insulted and will kill you with his sword. How can you respond to the situation? How do you stay alive?

Taking up kong-an, one is led into a dilemma. Once kong-an is entered, there is no going forward, no turning left, no turning right, and no turning back. There is only kong-an, unavoidable. Most people struggle with kong-ans. There is an inherent intimidation because kong-ans create a crisis for the linear, discursive mind. Throughout our whole life, we are educated in linear problem-solving: "If this, then that." We are indoctrinated at an early age in deduction and induction. We are taught to rely on memory and reason. We look to conventional wisdom and science for an explanation of the phenomena of life. Kong-an confronts this mind. Conventional reason is challenged, revealing original mind, the mind of true self.

Holding the question, the conditioned mind falls away, and something bright and boundless is revealed. And not satisfied with the "boundless," the conditioned mind probes the question deeper until all bliss and special states are resolved, and we see the world just as it is. The mind is bright and clear, and everything is reflected as it appears, "just like this," without distortion. How then can you reflect the sound of one hand clapping?

Although kong-an practice was formalized in China, Shakyamuni Buddha's first practice was the kong-an "Who am I?" The Buddha was a prince who lived a very protected life. One day he saw a dead person and realized how limited his view of the world was. Seeing that this life is impermanent was a challenge to his linear mind. "If we die, then what does it mean to live?" In this way, as we all do, he encountered the original human kong-an "Who am I?"

Shakyamuni left the safety of the palace and went out into the world to find an answer. He studied with many different holy men until finally, exhausted, he sat down with his question and took up the matter himself. He looked into the question of life and death. One morning he saw a star, and his mind burst open. He realized his true self; he became enlightened. To become enlightened means to see things as they are, to realize the "just like this" of our existence.

It is easy to come to some realization. It is difficult to manifest that realization, moment by moment.

Kong-an study is not separate from our everyday life. I am good friends with a certain couple. The husband is a physician and the wife boards horses. He is intellectual and has always relied upon his ability to think through a situation or problem. In fact, as a physician, his training has exploited these characteristics maximally. She, on the other hand, is quite passionate and has relied more upon her feelings for her direction, her understanding, and decision making. As one who works with horses, she has a "feel" for the animal and responds accordingly. In Jungian terms, he would be a "thinking type" and she would be a "feeling type." Opposites, yet compatible. They are both religiously devout and have been guided in their life together by traditional Western religious beliefs and practice. Recently, their eighteen-year-old son died from heart failure. He had a congenital heart disease but was living a normal life. Even though we knew Andrew would perhaps die earlier than his peers, no one expected it so soon.

We don't expect death. Even though we all "know" everyone is going to die "someday," we don't know when. It is the kong-an of our life. Human beings have many beliefs that try to address the problem of death, that try to ease the pain. But when it happens, especially out of sequence, we are startled, and the linear mind is thrown into conflict. People who have lived a long time die. That's the way life is. Because of our ideas about life, and contrary to nature's insistence, we believe fathers and mothers are supposed to die before their sons and daughters. Children and young people shouldn't die even if they are sick. It seems to violate a natural order.

With the death of their son, my friends were thrown into a crisis. They were confronted with a life kong-an that didn't make sense. This morning, Andrew was alive, active, and energetic. Right now, he is dead, still, and

quiet. Why? The explanation "Because he had heart disease" doesn't solve it or put it to rest. His early death
confronted everyone who knew him with a multitude of
questions. It exposed the impermanence of existence as
unavoidable fact.

My friends speak of the experience of being with
Andrew's body, of spending their entire time in the
funeral home and then in the church where Andrew was
laid out for visitation—just being with the body. They
didn't sleep or even want to. Nor did they leave their
son's side until he was buried. Unable to avoid or change
the fact of Andrew's death, they could only dwell on it.

It was a profound meditation, and they were both
deeply opened by the experience. For the next several
days, they simply glowed. For long lines of visiting
friends, they were compassionate, warm, and receptive.
They were able to respond to others, and people seemed
buoyed by their grace. In the time following Andrew's
death, they were the compassionate ones, giving to all
who came toward them.

Since this opening, they have begun to meditate
daily. Having experienced the transcendent, they are
drawn to manifest it and extend it to this boundless
Universe. They have been able to use this unbearable
event as a spiritual experience and as a precipitant for
going beyond. They found no fixed answers to the
meaning of life and death during those days with
Andrew's body. What they found was the need to enter
not-knowing without hesitation and without hope for a
permanent conclusion. The result of their opening to
not-knowing mind was undifferentiated compassion.

As hundreds of people came to say good-bye to Andrew and offer their condolences, each one was greeted by two people who were alive, immediate, and responsive, neither denying their grief nor encumbered by it. Waiting in the receiving line for two hours, I watched the grieving parents meet many people, all of whom had varied reactions to Andrew's death and their loss. No matter what each particular mourner came with, my friends patiently met each without judgment, listened, and then went on to the next person in line. They had embraced the kong-an of Andrew's death. Living in the midst of it, they glowed with compassion and illuminated this whole world.

Resistance as Kong-An Practice

The core of kong-an practice is the student-teacher relationship. While our Western psychological minds tend to see these relationships in terms of psychoanalytic transference (the projection of incomplete relationships from childhood, especially those with parents, onto the teacher), this is not a very helpful model. While transference issues certainly arise, they tend to be nonproductive and to distract rather than facilitate. Kong-an practice requires a singular focus.

The first kong-an in formal kong-an practice is our relationship to kong-an practice itself, our resistance to the not-knowing mind. There is resistance to being seen as we are. There is a fear of being seen as a fool. To not-know is to feel foolish. We spend most of our lives trying to avoid this feeling, learning to overcome the feeling that we are limited in our ability to know truth through thought. Yet not-knowing is our fundamental ground of being. It is our very life source.

Another resistance to kong-an practice is our desire for approval. Because we want the approval of the teacher, we fear that by not answering a kong-an correctly, we expose our vulnerability and lose his or her approval. Yet in true spiritual practice, there is no safety. It demands everything. We must expose ourselves completely, with all our inadequacies, and accept the consequences.

An old master calls to his attendant, "Attendant, bring me my rhinoceros fan!"

The attendant answers, "But Master, you know the rhinoceros fan is broken."

"Then bring me the rhinoceros!"

The old master wants the attendant as he is, broken horn and all. The enlightened mind is not special. It cannot be attained by special adjustment. Present yourself as you are, without hesitation. Entering kong-an is great courage. Staying with kong-an through fear and boredom is great faith. Attaining kong-an is great compassion.

Dongshan's "Going Beyond Buddha"

The Chinese Master Dongshan once taught, "Concerning realization through the body of going beyond Buddha, I would like to talk a little."

A monk said, "What is this talk?"

Dongshan said, "When I talk, you don't hear it."

The monk asked, "Can you hear it, Master?"

Then Dongshan replied, "Wait until I don't talk, then you will hear."

Inquiry

1. What is the meaning of going beyond Buddha? What is the meaning of going beyond? What is the meaning of Buddha?

2. Having gone beyond Buddha, what then do we become?

3. What is the meaning of "When I talk, you don't hear it"?

4. What is the meaning of "Wait until I don't talk, then you will hear"?

Author's Commentary

Going beyond,
Going beyond,
Going beyond.
Don't look back!
White flowers in spring,
Red berries in the fall.

Dongshan was a ninth-century Chinese Zen master. This exchange took place more than eleven hundred years ago. It is interesting that even after a thousand years, this dialogue between student and teacher is still relevant.

Our American culture is very, very new. At this time in America, we are influenced by pop fads and institutions designed for instant gratification. What seems to be evolving here in America—which is somewhat disheartening—is a kind of McDonald's Zen, a drive-through Zen. Pick up your enlightenment on the way to the movies. And if practice causes the slightest discomfort, dissatisfaction, unhappiness, give it a thumbs down and move on.

Zenkei Shibayama, a contemporary Japanese Zen master, in *Zen Comments on the Mumonkan,* says, "Man [we can say human] once and for all has to be driven to the abyss of dualistic contradiction and completely die to his small self in the depths of spiritual struggle. Unless he is reborn, breaking through this barrier, he cannot be really free in living his actual everyday life."*

Unless we truly die in this life, unless we are willing to completely die, to end, without hope of continuity or salvation, there can be no freedom. There is simply the past continuing on in a chain of continuity and mediocrity.

Again and again and again, our lives pit us against the irreconcilable. We have wants. We long. We desire, and our desires are never completely satisfied. They are satisfied for a moment, but in the moment of satisfaction,

---

*Shibayama, Zenkei, *Zen Comments on the Mumonkan* (New York: Harper and Row, 1975), p. 306.

the longing only increases. Daitsu Chisho Buddha sat in the temple for ten *kalpas*. Buddha-dharma was not manifest, and he did not become Buddha. *Daitsu* means "the one who had attained at all phases the no-nature, no-self reality of all things." *Chisho* means "the one who does not rely on any teaching and has no doubt whatsoever under any circumstances." A monk asked Master Seijo, "If this is so, why did he not become Buddha?" Seijo answered, "What a splendid question. Thank you for your wonderful question." But the monk persisted. "He practiced meditation for ten kalpas on the *bodhi* seat. Why did he not attain Buddhahood?" And Seijo answered, "Because he did not become Buddha."

From our ordinary way of thinking, we say that going beyond Buddha means I am here, Buddha is above me, and I will surpass him. In Zen lineage, transmission is always described as standing on the head of your teacher. The true transmission does not take place until you are standing on the head of your teacher. And so from the mind of measurement, we think "better than," going beyond Buddha is becoming better than Buddha. To receive transmission is to "best" your teacher. Because we are competitive, we compete in every manner, shape, and form possible. There can be competition in everything from cockroach and frog races to being the best in school or the top executive at work. Even in our Zen practice, we begin to measure ourselves, one against another. "He is more awake than she is. She is always falling asleep in the Dharma room." When I practiced at one particular monastery, the students took great pride in the quality of their sitting and would measure one another, and spur one another on, to sit better, to best one another in the meditation hall. Conversations were filled with comparison: whose samadhi was stronger and more intense?

At first glance, to "go beyond Buddha" appears to be this kind of besting Buddha. But if we look into the notion of Buddha, what is Buddha? What does it mean, *Buddha? Buddha* in Buddhist terms means "one who is awake, and who is enlightened, an enlightened one, an awakened one." One who is completely and totally awake. But what does it mean to be awake? We have images and ideas, but what is the attainment of being awake, and how is being awake demonstrated?

At its basis, listening is pure emptiness. *Shunyata.* Bright and shiny, fertile and void. A Buddha is one whose mind is pure and lucid and whose light penetrates the Dharma world. How could anyone go beyond that? In fact, *Buddha* means "one who has gone beyond." One who has gone to the other shore to attain Buddha-hood. One who has gone beyond this ordinary way of thinking, this small-self way of seeing the world and who is manifesting as the world itself. How do we go beyond this? Yet go beyond it we must.

To hold on to anything, even the most sacred, is to fix a position; and from that fixation, suffering arises. In the Heart Sutra (Appendix 3), we chant at the end, "*Gate, gate, paragate, parasamgate, bodhi svaha.*" One translation of this is "Gone, gone, gone beyond, gone beyond the great beyond, alleluia." This is the meaning of going beyond Buddha, going beyond going beyond.

Our practice is to go beyond going beyond going beyond, going beyond. No resting place anywhere.

Buddha is everything. Sky is Buddha. Tree is Buddha. You are Buddha. I am Buddha. Floor is Buddha. Altar is Buddha. Mat is Buddha. Dog is Buddha. All things are Buddha. Going beyond all of that is going beyond going beyond. Holding nothing, abiding nowhere, we say, living the homeless life. To live homelessly is to abide nowhere, and it means to die. To die in each moment, to die in each moment; to be reborn, fresh, alive, with no continuity. This is not something you can bring about at will but is a reality that is fundamental to all of us.

What is it that keeps us from realizing going beyond? What is the cause of our sticking? I don't mean to answer this in an analytical way, in a way that intends to resolve and get over being stuck. I don't mean to become dualistic and oppose the stuckness. But what is the nature of getting stuck? What is the nature of expectation, and how is it that expectation keeps us locked into a particular perspective? What is the barrier to going beyond Buddha, going beyond self-interest and a fixed perspective—going beyond how we think things should be?

What is *primary cause*?

Perhaps when we are practicing, we have some moment of clarity when the clouds dissipate and blue sky manifests everywhere, clear and unencumbered. Blue sky everywhere. And how sweet this glorious nirvana is. How truly joyous this lack of hindrances. We all have some moment. Each of us has tasted it somewhere in our lives, some moment of ease. This is ease of being, ease of going beyond, ease of unstuckness, where the constant struggle both inside and outside just quiets for a moment. We stop blaming someone. We stop longing for something or someone. We are just alive in the moment. We have gone beyond all idea of how it should be.

But this feeling doesn't last. Self-consciousness appears, and the magical intimacy vanishes.

What do we do when self-consciousness sets in? What do we do when thought intrudes and when memories from the past interfere with clarity? What do we do when clouds roll into the blue sky, when the joy is no longer cloudless? The thunder is roaring and the lightning is flashing, and we are lost in the storm of our own ambition, longing, disappointment, depression, sadness, and frustration. What do we do when we're no longer clear?

The sun shines everywhere, why does a cloud obscure it? Clouds move in, clouds move out, and the condition of the sky never changes. Whatever the content of sky, sky never changes. Whether our intimacy in drinking a cup of tea is clear and without hindrance, or whether we are bothered by all kinds of longing, it all takes place in the context of the great sky. When we are listening, listening to a friend talk, or listening to the screech of nails on a blackboard, even though we prefer one over the others, that listening is the sky. What is heard is what passes through this great, vast, immutable, empty sky, which is our fundamental nature.

Going beyond Buddha means *don't check* anything.

And if the checking mind appears, don't check that either. Going beyond Buddha means *don't hold* anything back. Going beyond Buddha means, whatever you are doing, *just do it*. If you do it with self-consciousness and thought, just do it anyway. If you do it with clarity and compassion, don't check that either, because that will become a sticking point in your going beyond. Simply, moment by moment, whatever you are doing, do that. And whatever condition your sky is, in the going beyond, in the enlightenment of your moment, don't check yourself. Let all expectation drop away. Whatever is in front of you, that is Buddha. Whatever you are doing is the activity of enlightenment. The name for this is *annutara samyak sambodhi*: everywhere and always, completely and totally enlightened. This realization is *primary cause*.

Once a monk was standing at the altar after having a deep and profound satori. A young monk came up to him and said, "Wow, you have become enlightened. You've had a break, an opening. Your mind is clear and wide. How is it?" And the monk said, "Miserable as ever."

Zen Master Kyong Ho, just before he died, wrote the following poem:

> *The moon of clear mind drinks up everything.*
> *When moon and mind disappear,*
> *What is this?*

Splendid. Going beyond even the clarity of clarity. Going beyond the moon of clear mind. Going beyond drinking up everything. What is this? This going beyond going beyond.

Another great Zen master, at the very moment of his death, took out his pen and wrote the following lines:

> *I don't want to die.*
> *I don't want to die.*
> *I don't want to die.*

We are both these states. Both holding and letting go. Without clarity, there is no delusion. Without delusion, there is no clarity. We are both. We must go beyond both. Going beyond both doesn't mean resolving or working through or getting over or getting better or acquiring or attaining or achieving. Going beyond means simply going beyond. Going beyond means whatever you are doing just now, only do it.

How is it that we get stuck?

Because the nature of our existence is all-inclusive, there is really no sticking place. Because the nature of our mind is such that it includes everything, there is really no place to get stuck. Because the nature of who we are is to complete all that there is, there is no sticking point. That is the meaning of going beyond Buddha. Not something to be attained, but something to wake up to, again and again. If we wake up to the fact that we idealize and struggle and oppose, we accept that as well. If we simply wake up to the fact that we are distracted by our own thought habits, we accept that too. If we wake up to the fact that we are mean and dark and controlling and demanding and emotional and leaking all over the place with our dissatisfactions, with our own inner condition, we accept that also. Not opposing anything. Accepting everything. We are alive. Our future is here and now. If we cannot endure this moment, when and where will we?

Man Gong's "In the Sound of the Bell"

One day Zen Master Man Gong said, "All Zen masters say that in the sound of the bell they attain enlightenment, and at the sound of the drum they fall down. Anyone who understands the meaning of this, please give me an answer."

A student named Song Wol stood up and said, "If the rabbit's horn is correct, the sheep's horn is false."

Man Gong smiled.

Zen Master Seung Sahn's comment: "If you cannot hear the bell or the drum, you are free. If you hear both sounds, you are already in hell."

Inquiry

1. What is the meaning of "all Zen masters say they attain enlightenment in the sound of the bell and fall down at the sound of the drum"?

2. What is the meaning of "When the rabbit's horn is correct, the sheep's horn is false"?

3. What is the meaning of Man Gong's smile?

Zen Master Man Gong said, "All Zen masters say that in the sound of the bell they attain enlightenment, and at the sound of the drum they fall down." What is the meaning of attaining enlightenment? What is the meaning of falling down? Are the meanings of attaining enlightenment and falling down the same, or are they different? If you say they are the same, you are lost in oneness. If you say they are different, you miss the very point. How are these two points reconciled?

All Zen masters say that in the sound of the bell, they attain enlightenment. Notice that Man Gong is not saying *because of* the sound of the bell, but *in the very sound of* the bell itself, all Zen masters attain enlightenment. At the very sound of the drum they fall down. What, indeed, is the difference between attaining and falling down? Do they fall down completely? The complete falling of falling down? The sound of the bell and the sound of the drum—are they the same or are they different? From one point of view, they originate from the same source, from no sound at all. Sound arises from no-sound. Emptiness. From one perspective, the sound of the bell and the sound of the drum are exactly the same. From another perspective, the sound of the bell and the sound of the drum are quite different. And yet, Zen Master Seung Sahn says, if you hear either, you fall into hell. What can you do if you make the mistake of hearing the sound of the bell and the sound of the drum? What can you do if you find yourself in the hell realm of having heard something? How does hearing something differ from listening?

Life is falling down and getting up. Falling down,

getting up. Falling down, getting up. Falling down, getting up. Falling down, getting up. Falling down, getting up. When we see our lives from a certain perspective of aspiration, we see that falling down is a response to certain circumstances. Perhaps we are in psychotherapy and want to get over our anxiety or our nuances of personality caused by early trauma. We are stuck in our consciousness, and this seems to affect things in daily life. If only we could get over something. We want to get over the falling down of our lives, the mistakes. So we go about examining, evaluating, considering changes and working through, deconditioning, extinguishing, resolving our falling down. And yet Man Gong says that at the sound of the drum, all great Zen masters fall down.

When people used to tell Zen Master Seung Sahn that they felt crazy, he would say, "Yes, become completely crazy." That means falling down is complete. In complete falling down, there is no falling and no getting up. It is only the partial, or fragmented, life that is a life of suffering. There is an old Zen adage that goes "When killing, be sure you see the blood."

This kong-an points to how the linear mind is conditioned to see things in a *causal* way. Something happens, and something else occurs because of it. Somehow, the sound of the bell will bring about a state called enlightenment. It calls enlightenment to come into being. When we are in a particular state of mind that is not very becoming to us, not very satisfying, not complete, we seek something outside ourselves, like the sound of the bell, to bring us into another state, to create something different from what we are experiencing. To enlighten us. To lighten us. So there is hope that there will be some kind of intervention, that we will be saved from our suffering in some way. We may look to certain groups of people, like Zen masters, because our karma is Zen Buddhist. It could be desert fathers, gurus, Ph.D.'s, elementary-school teachers, parents, our mothers and fathers, our friends. We look toward them. We tend automatically to set ourselves apart from certain groups of people and presume that they have something that we do not. We idealize them and become bitterly disappointed when we find that they fall down too. And sometimes these presumptions, especially in regard to parents, are so subtle and so unconscious that we don't even know we have them.

All Zen masters say that in the sound of the bell, they fall down and at the sound of the drum, they get up. Falling down, getting up. Attaining, not attaining. Losing, gaining. Having, not having. Coming and going. What does it all add up to?

There are two mountains. Which one is the true mountain? All Zen masters say in the sound of the bell, attain enlightenment. At the sound of the drum, fall down. Bell and drum. Which one is best? Would you rather attain enlightenment or attain falling down? Which would you prefer? Would you choose enlightenment over falling down? Or do you choose falling down over enlightenment? And after enlightenment and falling down, then what?

Man Gong is saying the true Zen master gets enlightenment and falls down. Thus, there is no attainment of an ideal state to dwell in forever. There is no mistake to have to pay for in an eternity of suffering. It is only when we are worried about our particular life condition that suffering arises. When we live our big life, we make only big mistakes, which are only for all beings. Then falling down and enlightenment are the same coin, different sides. But this is all explanation. How can you demonstrate your realization of enlightenment and falling down, just here and just now?

The second door to this kong-an is the monk's comment "If the rabbit's horn is correct, the sheep's horn is false." This means if the turtle's hair is correct, then the lion's hair is not correct. Form is form, emptiness is emptiness. If the palm appears, the fist disappears. Cause and effect cannot be avoided even in enlightenment. Once there was a Zen master who was asked, "Does an enlightened man fall out of the realm of cause and effect?" He answered, "Yes," and had to live in a fox's body for five hundred lifetimes. He was later freed by the turning phrase of another Zen master: "An enlightened man is not separate from cause and effect." Both Zen masters were wrong. Why?

Wind blows, white clouds separate.
Rain falls, trees grow up.

And finally, what is the meaning of Man Gong's smile? Is Man Gong approving or placating or merely agreeing? On one occasion, Shakyamuni Buddha was supposed to give a lecture at Vulture Peak. Hundreds of devotees came to hear the talk, to hear the truth spoken by a buddha. Shakyamuni Buddha was silent for a long time; then he held up a flower. He didn't say a word. If you really want to hear the Dharma, listen to this flower.

No one in the audience understood, except for one old monk, Mahakasyapa. Because Mahakasyapa had come to realization, he could hear with his eyes and see with his nose. He lived without hindrance. And so Mahakasyapa only smiled. Seeing Mahakasyapa smile, Buddha said, "Oh! Only Mahakasyapa understands. So I transmit my true, incomparable, profound Dharma to him."

Using the story as a point of inquiry, we ask, "Was Mahakasyapa's smile the same or different from Man Gong's smile in this kong-an?" Also, the Buddha made a big mistake when he said, "I transmit my true Dharma to you, Mahakasyapa." What was the Buddha's mistake, and how do you make it correct, without explanation? If you were there at that time, what could you do?

Then, there is Zen Master Seung Sahn's comment: "If you cannot hear the bell or the drum, you are free. If you hear both sounds you are already in hell."

When our consciousness is discriminating this from that, when it is comparing, how can we possibly know God? It is our human tendency constantly to think one thing is better than another. What if we make the great mistake of falling into hell? What can we do? *Help the demons.* Whatever circumstance we find ourselves in, it is a potential heaven realm. When the like-dislike mind, the judging, evaluating mind, is dominant, even the most serene circumstance becomes a source of suffering. By cutting off the mind of evaluation, even the worst situation is transformed and the gates of heaven open. Hell is transformed not by changing our circumstances but by realizing our human direction.

There has never been a period without war in human history. We live in conflict. We are attached to our opinions and ideas. As a consequence, our fellow beings suffer. So if you fall into hell and are confronted by demons every day, what can you do?

There is an old story about heaven and hell. Hell is described as a gourmet banquet with all the choice foods available in abundance. All the people in hell have four-foot utensils glued to their fingers such that they cannot get food to their mouths. The tables are turned over, the food is ruined and spread all over the place. It is chaos. Heaven is exactly the same situation, except that the inhabitants are feeding one another.

> *This whole world is turning, turning, turning.*
> *Before this world existed there was only silence.*
> *After this world disappears, only silence.*
> *Silence before, silence after.*
> *Then where does sound come from?*
> *Katz!*
> *Baby cries, whaa, whaa, whaa.*
> *Here is some milk.*

Ko Sahn's "Knowing How to Hit the Drum"

Zen Master Ko Sahn, instructing a group of monks, said, "Studying is called listening. Cutting off study is called nearness. Past these two is true passing."

A monk came forward and asked, "What is true passing?"

"Knowing how to hit the drum," Ko Sahn replied.

The monk asked, "And what is real truth?"

"Knowing how to hit the drum."

The monk continued, "Mind is Buddha. I'm not asking about this. What is no-mind, no-Buddha?"

"Knowing how to hit the drum."

"And when a transcendent person comes, how do you receive that person?"

"Knowing how to hit the drum."

Knowing how to hit the drum is an interesting Zen pointer. All of us are born knowing how to hit the drum, but through countless kalpas of karma we become lost in a haze of conceptualization. We become identified with the stuff of our life, our thoughts, our concepts. It is like going to a symphony and not listening to the whole thing but rather identifying with a few notes, or paying more attention to what the musicians are wearing than listening to what they are playing. To identify with any of the notes in the symphony or any one part is to miss the point, to miss the whole, to not know how to hit the drum.

Can there be a transformation from *identifying* as the content of listening, of seeing, of smelling, of tasting, of touching, and of thinking, to a *realization of the moment* of listening, seeing, smelling, tasting, touching, and thinking? Can consciousness transform, realizing that the tendency to fixate on impermanent phenomena is an error? Sound arises, sound dwells, sound disappears. Our life is just like this. In a moment a friend appears; we reach out and touch, then withdraw; the friend is gone. It is only memory that holds on to that friend. Seeing into this matter, we find a new friend and a new friend and a new friend in every moment. Everything met is brand-new. Every moment touched is brand-new, a fresh sound never before heard. Having died to the last moment, everything is born in this moment. To die and be born, to die and be born, to die and be born forever.

There is no need to rely upon memory, for memory is inherently unreliable, an ever-shifting distortion. Likewise, there is no need to rely on preconceived notions of how things should be or of what is best. There is no need to create expectations based upon how we were raised, what others want for us, or what we hope to have or to avoid. Believing that we can understand, predict, and describe is a psychological virus that invades our thinking. In some contexts, prediction is necessary. For example, we need to know which car to choose in the parking lot, or if we want to use a computer, we need to learn how. But attachment to concepts seeps through and infiltrates every aspect of our consciousness like a fog. The virus of knowing. A set of phenomena arise, and it reminds us of another set. So we begin to label it this way or that way, and the whole process of "being-with" loses its aliveness. There is fear and withholding. We begin to identify whatever process we are in with processes from the past. We hold on to the past and live through it.

Try listening to sound as one would listen to the birds. Don't create anything. Only allow all sounds—irritating sounds as well as melodious sounds—to be what they are. Don't make anything special, anything different. Don't move from it at all: not toward it, not away from it. It's happening in this present moment. A sound is occurring, and we need no effort at all to hear it, to listen. It requires no effort at all. No will, no ego-intervention. One doesn't have to remember what it sounded like or worry about how long it will continue. One doesn't have to have a relationship with it in a cognitive, abstract, or conceptual way. Relationship is already there; it is immediate. Don't create anything. Just listen.

This is the first aspect of listening, the oneness of listening. There is oneness. There is intimacy. But how does intimacy function? We have in our school a practice, during the interview, in which a student comes in and the teacher says, "Where are you coming from?" The student hits the floor with his or her hand. "Where are you coming from?" Another hit. That is the demonstration of oneness, becoming one. Whenever anyone asked Zen Master Ma Jo a question, he hit them. Whenever anyone asked Zen Master Lin Chi a question, he shouted, "Katz!" When anyone asked Zen Master Guji a question, he held up one finger. All responses demonstrate this one point. Hit! The sound and you are one. Two beings listening to the same sound, not separate. When you are thinking, there is separation. When you cut off all thinking [hit!!], all things are realized as one.

But we can't function like that. There must be some particular expression of this oneness as the wide variety of phenomena arise. If a child is about to run into the street, what do we do? If the child is about to run into the street after a ball, how do we manifest? If we just abide in oneness with *hit* or *Katz,* the child would be killed. Our listening needs one more step. And if our listening is clear, pure listening, we "know how to hit the drum" of each situation. When someone comes who is hungry, we feed him; when someone comes who is tired, we give her a place to sleep. If a child has a nightmare, we soothe him. If an adult has a nightmare, we help her to face her own demons.

The following is a dialogue that developed at a retreat held at Gethsemani Abbey.

DAE GAK: What is the meaning of truth? Knowing how to hit the drum. And so, what is the meaning of knowing how to hit the drum? Who can answer? [*Pause—followed by a rap on the floor by one present.*] That's knowing how to hit the floor! [*Laughter.*] So what is the true meaning of knowing how to hit the drum? Now you see our mind is quite complicated, and we take it from a metaphysical standpoint that knowing how to hit the drum means our true self. And, indeed, in some ways it does mean our true self. But is our true self separate from its phenomenon? How could it be? We don't say that is our true self over there, and its phenomenon is over here. Speaking metaphorically, we say, "What is our true self?" "Knowing how to hit the drum"—what does this mean?

RETREATANT: I would think that it is in losing yourself.

D.G.: You would *think* that. [*Laughter.*]

R: When you see a good drummer.

D.G.: But that's knowing how to appreciate a good drummer. So if you see someone who is really a good drummer, and you see him playing, and you go, "Ah! Wonderful!" that's knowing how to appreciate someone who hits the drum. But, indeed, what is it for each of us?

R.: I would say that it means living in the present moment.

D.G.: Sure, those are all the descriptions of knowing how to hit the drum, living in the present moment, abiding in the now, living in the now, abiding in God, abiding in Buddha-mind, abiding in Christ's love, all of those describe it. But what is knowing how to hit the drum? If we embrace the kong-an, not going left, not going right, not making any deviation at all, staying right on the mark, then what? [*Laughter.*]

R.: [*Makes movement with her hand.*]

D.G.: Only this?

R.: *Boom.*

D.G.: So knowing how to hit the drum is so simple and straightforward, and yet we make it complicated, make it second-level understanding.

Knowing how to hit the drum. It is so simple, yet we lose our clarity and follow our thinking. Can we find the correct "hitting of the drum" in every situation we encounter?

In the Christian tradition, we say that we do not

depend on anything but God. But if we see God as something separate from ourselves, we make God an idea. God becomes a creation in our own minds. Thus, we depend on an image of God, not God itself. Our practice is to abide in—listening. How can you hear the word of God?

R.: Would you repeat what you said about the cardinal?

D.G.: When Zen Master Seung Sahn came to Kentucky for the first time, he saw cardinals and said, "Oh, that's Avalokitesvara, the Bodhisattva of Compassion." So every time a cardinal would come, he'd say, "Oh, Kwan Se Um Bosal" [the Korean name for Avalokitesvara].

R.: If the teaching is life as it is, reality as it is, then the goal of practice is to see what is in each moment. Reality, or life, is always communicating itself clearly. And the human dilemma is that we don't see that. Is it not accurate that the karma eye that is formed is the reason why we don't see? Would you agree with that?

D.G.: Let's see if we can change that a little bit into a question. Your statement was "The goal of Zen practice is to see reality as it is, and the karma eye is the reason that we can't see reality as it truly exists." OK. Let's pose it as a question. What is reality? What is the karma eye? Who is it that sees? Who is it that can't see? Let's not come to some conclusion about it.

R.: You said that earlier, that you can't hear in the past, and you can't hear in the future, and I was following you there, and I said that you can hear in the present, and you said, "No, you can't hear in the present either."

D.G.: The present is only an idea.

R.: So do you make any difference between this moment and the present?

D.G.: Well, for purposes of pointing, yes. There is no moment. There is only—[*sound of clapper sticks*]. We say, "Past mind cannot hear that, present mind cannot hear that, future mind cannot hear that." Why? These are concepts. But how do you cut off all concepts?

R.: [*Claps hands.*] [*Laughter.*]

D.G.: But concepts are our life. To cut them off, you have to have a lot of faith. We've been relying on concepts up till now, and they've done a pretty good job, right? But there's something, always something not quite right, not complete.

R.: Is that what Scripture is talking about when it says we are looking through a dim reflection in the mirror, but when we get to Heaven, we will see clearly?

D.G.: So, where is Heaven? Past mind cannot go to Heaven, future mind cannot go to Heaven, present mind cannot go to Heaven. Where is Heaven? Looking out the window into Heaven, "Ah, green trees, blue sky." But you know our linear mind wants to make Heaven somewhere else. We are here and we're going to go there, up in the sky, to Heaven, in the future.

R.: Is there any meaning to the word *now*?

[*The monastery bells ringing in the distance. Dae Gak Sunim cups his ear with his hand.*]

D.G.: What does *now* mean to you?

R.: *Now* means now. [*Bells stop ringing.*]

D.G.: Well, can you hear the bells?

R.: When they're ringing. [*Laughter.*]

D.G.: But that's not now. That's then. Listening is

constant. We are born listening. Even if we have no ears, we are born listening. We listen with our bodies and our bones. We are listening. So even though the bell has stopped ringing, you can still hear it. Listening doesn't come and go. The sound of the bell comes and goes, but listening is eternal. You are born into listening. When you die, listening will continue. There is a kong-an that emerges, "When you die, and your body goes to the cemetery, what happens to listening?"

R.: You make it sound so simple and straightforward. Why then is there suffering?

D.G.: Why is there suffering? If everything is so straightforward and simple, why is that humans are unhappy? What are we seeking, anyway? Why aren't we just living our lives, sipping lemonade on the porch? I understand that it is simple. I see the sky is blue and the tree is green. No need to suffer anymore. No need to strive for anything.

At first, we have a realization. "I get it! It's so simple! Only, *don't know!*" Then we realize the sky is blue and the grass is green. But one more step is necessary. How does our *don't know* function for all beings? So all beings suffer for you. How do you save them? *Knowing how to hit the drum!*

Tosu's "All Sounds Are Buddha's Sounds"

A monk asked Tosu, "All sounds are the sounds of Buddha. Right or wrong?"

Tosu said, "Right."

The monk said, "Master, doesn't your asshole make farting sounds?"

Tosu then hit him.

Again the monk asked, "Coarse words or subtle talk, all return to the primary meaning. Right or wrong?"

Tosu said, "Right."

The monk then said, "Then can I call you an ass, Master?"

Tosu hit him.

Are the sounds of farting, regurgitating, belching, different from the sounds of wind, birds, and rain on the roof? Are they not all the song of Kwan Se Um Bosal? Isn't it true that every sound, no matter how coarse or subtle, is the pure song of the Buddha, of Avalokitesvara, of God, of angels? The practice of listening makes no distinction in sound and realizes the source of all sound. Once one has realized the source of sound, everything becomes pure and clear. Sound is heard just as it is. But it is difficult to live in this realm.

Joju's Mu kong-an points to this checking mind.

A monk asked Zen Master Joju, "Does a dog have Buddha-nature?"

Joju said, "Mu!" ("No!")

This monk may have had an opening. But his realization was tender, so he began to check. He began to analyze. What about dogs? In China, dogs are considered low class. Perhaps we might say, "What about maggots or pigs or something socially unacceptable?" Or, more heinous, "What about mortar explosions and machine-gun fire? Do they have Buddha-nature?"

"Mu!"

Zen Master Seung Sahn once attended a large meeting where there was much talking and discussion. Two monks who attended him complained that it was boring and very intellectual. Zen Master Seung Sahn replied, "Because we are interested in all sentient beings, we go. We make no discrimination. We go and we listen without attachment to our opinion. We listen as one would listen to songs on the radio."

All sounds are the sounds of Buddha. It is interesting that we are ashamed of certain sounds. All of this is meaning put on sound, discrimination put on sound. From the point of view of the Absolute, to discriminate in sound is a big mistake, just as to discriminate in thought is a big mistake. The teaching is that when you are thinking, your mind and my mind are separate. But if we cut off all thinking, then your mind and my mind are not different. Without thinking, what is the meaning of farts, arguments, and gunshots?

Hearing the sound of the temple bell.
How can we stop the sound of the temple bell?

Having some realization of oneness is not enough. There is always the tendency for a particular realization to become conceptual because it is temporary. By holding on to the memory of a realization, the practice of realization is lost.

There is a story about a teacher and a student on a walk together. On a retreat, the student had an opening, an awakening, a *kensho*, clear mind. After the retreat, they walked back through the woods from the temple. The student looked at the leaves on the ground and said, "Look! Even those leaves on the ground have Buddha-nature!" They went a little farther and he said, "That tree over there has Buddha-nature!" "The squirrel has Buddha-nature." On and on and on. "Even the grass has Buddha-nature!" Finally, in exasperation, the teacher answered, "Yes, yes. Of course it's true, but you don't have to go announcing it at every turn!" Oneness, without the realization of its function for all beings, turns into self-centered activity.

After we have realized the oneness of sound, one more step is necessary. What is the correct function of this realization? Hearing our neighbors argue, how do we, without contamination by our own karma, respond to them? Without the violence of pacifism, how do we respond to the sounds of war? How do we sow harmony where there is adversity? When we hear a child cry, can we respond compassionately without overindulging it, neglecting it, or imposing our ideas of discipline on it? There are no easy answers. There are no formulas or doctrines that we can simply apply. This is the constant grist of our practice. Because the sky does not hold the clouds, the sun shines everywhere.

> *Two men are fighting on the other side of the river.*
> *You cannot get across, nor can they hear you if you yell.*
> *How do you stop them from fighting?*

Why Do We Put On the Seven-Fold Robe?

This world is vast and wide. Why then do you put on your seven-fold robe at the sound of the bell?

Traditionally, monks wear a seven-paneled robe when it is time to chant. Before they go to the chanting hall, they put on their seven-fold *kasa*. This kong-an is asking: If everything is one, why then at the sound of the bell do we put on our seven-fold robe? The sky is blue, the trees are green; why do we impose some arbitrary human condition or ritual?

If everything is one, if everything is Absolute, why do we put on the robe? Why do we follow forms? Why are there particular things we do in the world? Why have form? Why do we do spiritual practice? This whole world is vast and wide. Why practice at all? Form is emptiness, emptiness is form. Delusion is enlightenment, enlightenment is delusion. Why not just go about our way, eating rice and relieving ourselves when necessary, as Zen Master Lin Chi teaches?

Because one more step is necessary. You have one mouth, one nose, two eyes. Why do you have two eyes? Or you have two ears. Why do you have two ears?

This "why" is our greatest spiritual challenge. Why do you have two ears? Why were you born? Why do you live every day? Why do you eat every day? We have all practiced rituals in mindless ways in our life, done things in mindless ways because of tradition. We follow in the tradition in which we were raised. Our parents were Baptists, we are Baptists. Our parents were Buddhists, we follow them. Our parents gave us no spiritual direction, so we continue without direction.

"Why are you Buddhist?"

"Well, I was raised a Buddhist."

"Why are you Catholic?"

"I was raised a Catholic."

"Why are you getting good grades in school? Are you learning? Are you enjoying what you're doing?"

"I was raised to get good grades, it is expected of me."

"Why do you do poorly in school? Why do you do poorly in your life?"

"I had difficult times—a difficult life."

There is a tendency with this "why" question to blame, to point at something other than one's own direction as the cause. The question sets up a dualistic perspective. In relationships, "why" is almost always a dysfunctional statement. *Why do you talk to me that way? Why do you treat me that way? Why did you say this? Why did you say that? Why did you do this? Why did you do that?* "Why" often covers a disapproval: *I don't like it that you did this. I don't like it that you did that. Why do we have to chant? Why do we have to get up so early and practice?* The "why" covers an "I don't want to." Looking carefully, we see it is not sincere but marked with an agenda of its own.

Yet in another way, "why" is fundamental to our practice. It is the primary inquiry of all spiritual forms. Why? Why practice? Why come together to sit quietly? Why follow forms? Why try not to move? Why try to maintain an erect posture? Why chant? Why this chanting? Why not another chanting? These are very important questions. Why be successful? What is our motivation? Why take this spiritual direction?

We can look at anything we do in our lives with complete skepticism, raising this "why" question in an effort to search deeply. We must be careful to avoid the temptation to raise this question in a dysfunctional way, with a defensive intention, where the question itself implies disapproval. Instead, we raise this question in an open, skeptical, and inquiring way.

In Zen practice, the samadhi of immediacy develops. Someone calls your name. You respond, "Yes!"

Zen Master Song Am Eon used to call to himself and answer himself every day:

"Master!"

And he would answer, "Yes!"

"You must keep clear."

"Yes!"

"Never be deceived by others, any day, any time!!"

"Yes, yes."

Immediacy, not two. The call and the answer, one! The immediacy of living in the moment. The sound of the bell, putting on the robe. Don't doubt the sound of the *mok'tak*. Just do it. Don't check. The sound of the mok'tak, "Go to the Dharma room!" And don't follow blindly. What a challenge!

Whatever you're doing, then do it! Live life with unhesitating passion. Hearing the cries of the world, the suffering, and responding immediately, knowing exactly what to do. Being fully present to the sound of the bell. Putting on the robe. The bell rings, the robe goes on.

There is, of course, a potential danger in this. The danger is that one can begin to develop a set of rules to live by and then put one's life on automatic pilot. Eating at noon, having dinner at five, watching a couple of hours of TV, going to bed, waking up at six, shaving, having a bowel movement, maybe drinking a cup of coffee, and going off to work. Starting work at nine, at noon eating lunch with friends—there is a somnambulism, walking through one's life in a sleep state. Using the various schedules as signals for events, and mindlessly following them.

But because we question everything constantly and everywhere, keeping a not-knowing mind, we can respond with immediacy, alive in each moment.

At the sound of the bell, put on the seven-fold robe. Bell and robe and mind, put them all on at the same time. One, not separate. The sound of the bell is putting on the seven-fold robe. Not separate. It's not a signal now to put on the robe later. In full awareness, completely awake, we hear the sound of the bell and put on the robe. Not two actions but one complete act, hearing and putting on the robe.

The whole world is vast and wide. Why do we put on our seven-fold robe at the sound of the bell?

This "why" is the very heart of our practice. This "why" is the fundamental expression of our sitting and chanting. This "why." Our whole life is the question "why?" The energy of this question rolls up to the frontal lobes quickly, but if we can resist that, or at least see it, then we can remain, abide in the "why" itself. Why? Abide in it so it can penetrate every pore, every cell, every aspect of being—why—why? Why is the sky blue? Why do crows fly? Why? Not explained, but endlessly—why? Getting at the root of everything—why? Why? Do we have the courage to ask this question? To enter this question, leaving no trace of conclusion? In analysis, there is always the analyzer. In the true "why," there is no analyzer. Entering the "why" completely. WHY? There is only . . . ?

This whole world is vast and wide. Open your eyes, and you see it all. Listen, and you hear everything. One sound fills the myriad sense-worlds.

Once when I was riding with Zen Master Seung Sahn in the car, Mu Sang Sunim, a monk who travels with him regularly, was sound asleep in the back, his head bobbing. I said to Zen Master Seung Sahn, "Monk's job, sleeping in the car." He said to me, "Monk's job, perceiving this whole world."

Why perceive this world? This "whole world" kong-an is marvelous because it points to the varied aspects of enlightenment. First enlightenment: no self. Realization of oneness. And final enlightenment, realization of suchness, the "just like this"-ness of existence. At the sound of the bell, putting on the robe. At the sound of the tea kettle, pouring the water. Just like that.

Perceiving clearly, responding correctly. No more. No less.

We are indebted to those historic Zen masters who disrupted form in order to encourage perceiving the wider perspective. There is the story of Zen Master Wu Po, who visited the room in which all the monks were sitting quietly, eating in silence. In the middle of the meal, this serene, reverent meal, the master shouted, "KATZ!" and continued eating. The monks were disturbed, "Why did the master yell like that?"

We can analyze it and say that he was confronting their attachment to silence and reverence. One monk went to his master's room afterward, "Master, why did you yell during the meal? Was it because we were too attached to silence and reverence?"

The master yelled, "KATZ!"

Ching Ching's "Sound of Raindrops"

Ching Ching asked a monk, "What sound is that outside the gate?"

The monk said, "The sound of raindrops."

Ching Ching said, "Sentient beings are perverted. They lose themselves and follow things."

The monk said, "How about you, Master?"

Ching Ching said, "I almost don't lose myself."

The monk said, "What is the meaning of 'I almost don't lose myself'?"

Ching Ching said, "To explain is very easy. To reveal substance through speech is very difficult."

We have been using listening, the capacity to hear sound, as the point of entry into the river of Dharma. Ching Ching said to a monk, "What is that sound outside the gate?" Look at this very carefully. Ching is testing the monk. And I ask you, Is there a sound outside the gate?

We spend our whole lives believing there is an outside and an inside, that there is a gate that separates a fixed self, an "I," from something else that we call "not I." A wonderful example of this is that in your mouth, saliva is you. Spit into a glass and imagine drinking it. Your experience of the saliva shifts, because it is no longer in the body where you have been holding it. When it goes into the glass, the mind of separation appears, and the idea of drinking your saliva from a glass is distasteful, if not disgusting.

What is the sound that is outside the gate? In one way, this is a very straightforward question. In another way, in an equal way, this question is profound. What can possibly be heard outside the gate? Arbitrarily, we make the nose the gate of our breath: air on the one side of the body is an inhalation. Air on the other side of the nostril is an exhalation. That's the nose-gate. Inhalation and exhalation, an exchange.

All gates are arbitrary. Where do they come from? If you make a gate, you have a gate. If you don't make a gate, then you have no gate. What is the gate that is beyond gates, and how do you pass through the gate beyond all gates?

All gates depend on coming and going. It is in coming and going that gates appear. When coming and going no longer appear, then the gate has no front or back, no inside or outside.

We operate with the assumption of "I," and the assumption is such a constant habit that we are not even aware of it. We can't sense it. It pervades so much of what we do and experience, it is so automatic, that we don't even know that it is a creation of thought and memory. We call this construct "self" and believe in its permanence. It never gets called into question. Yet, because we are seekers of truth, we call everything into the question.

Imagine we are in a room together. Listen carefully to your thoughts: "I" am sitting on this cushion, talking. "You" are sitting on that cushion, listening. There is a certain amount of truth to that. But what is the "I" that is sitting, listening? Where does the gate fit that defines "I," the compound of "I," "the I fortress"? Does the gate of who you are rest in your ear? At the edge of your skin? Does it rest in the air between us? Does it rest in my vocal cords as the sounds are formed? Does it rest in our consciousness, where meaning is interpreted? Where is the gate of "self," of "I"? Where does this "I" come from and where does it go? Descartes said, "I think, therefore I am." Zen Master Seung Sahn says, "If you are not thinking, then what?"

Personal "I" appears like the moon reflected in the water. This reflection must not be taken for the moon itself. It would be like the manager of a baseball team thinking he was the owner. When baseball team managers start acting like owners, or stop doing their job, they get fired. One time a friend of mine visited Mother Teresa while she was sick in the hospital. There was a group of visitors, and each said a few kind words to the ailing nun. Finally it was my friend's turn, and she said, "Mother, thank you very much for your wonderful work with the poor and dying. You are truly an inspiration." The frail nun raised herself up, and with the roar of a lion said, "It is not *my* work! It is God's work!"

Ching Ching asks, "What sound is that outside the gate?"

The monk responds, "The sound of raindrops."

This is a big mistake, of course, and this monk swallows the hook for all beings, you and me. Ching Ching responds directly, reflecting what he perceives, "Sentient beings are perverted. They lose themselves and follow things." Ching Ching is reflecting the nature of the thinking mind, small mind. The tendency of the mind to try to explain, and the tendency of the mind to follow explanation. When a bone is thrown, a dog jumps up and chases after it, while a lion stays put and looks in the direction where the bone came from.

The master says, "Sentient beings are perverted. They lose themselves and follow things." The monk says, "How about you, Master?" Point one finger and three are pointed back. Ching, not missing a beat, responds, "I almost don't lose myself." I too am a sentient being and am lost in the weeds. There is one small difference: I know that I don't know. I almost don't lose myself. I know that I don't know.

When Bodhidharma, the legendary founder of Zen, confronted the Chinese Emperor Wu, Emperor Wu said, "Who are you?" Bodhidharma replied, "Bu shik." The Chinese calligraphy describing Bodhidharma's response is often translated as, "I don't know," but it is literally "not-knowing," or "no-knowing." Later Emperor Wu asked his teacher about this exchange and who Bodhidharma was. His teacher said, "Don't you know who that man was?" And Emperor Wu said, "I don't know!" These two "don't knows," Bodhidharma's and the emperor's, are they the same or different?

"I almost don't lose myself." I almost don't know. Almost not losing oneself is complete. It is the not-knowing that has no subject or object. It is the not-knowing that is clear and pervades the whole universe. It is the not-knowing that is unbounded, unfettered, uncluttered, and unclouded. It is the crystal-clear immediacy of this uninterpreted moment. It is quite a different affair from the "I don't know and I want to," where there is subject and object, where the construction of self continues, lost in thought or fantasy. For Ching, the self is almost formed, almost solidified, but only enough to be compassionate for you and me.

So the monk asks, "What is the meaning of 'I almost don't lose myself'?" And Ching really has to explain: "To explain is very easy. To reveal substance through speech is very difficult." So then speak! Please! Reveal substance, Master Ching!

Ching falls deep into the swamp of explanation, for you and for me. How can we get him out of the swamp? How to save Ching with words of substance, not explanation? How to save this whole world with words of substance, not dead words of explanation, not already used words, not other people's words, not words we've heard, or words we've read or learned, words we've been told or figured out? But with alive words, immediate words, words that express a truth that stops the entire world?

"To explain is very easy. To reveal substance through speech is very difficult." This is our life. We spend our adult life separate from our existence, analyzing, evaluating, reflecting, explaining, and describing. So little of our time on earth passes in actual, realized experience. (Hitting the floor, *whack!*). Do *you* hear that sound? What is the sound outside your ear-gate? Our life is simple, completely simple. Like the temple bell ringing in the empty sky. And yet we keep adding something to it. We add explanation. We add understanding, concentration, samadhi, special energy, or books on Zen. And when we add something to it, there is separation and dualism.

Zen teaching is clear: *put it all down*. Put down your opinion, your condition, and your situation. Let it all go, and come back to *this!* (*Whack!*) And when there is some experience of this, we have to let *that* go as well. And when there is an experience of the void, emptiness, the not-knowing mind, suchness, that too must be dropped or it becomes a memory, a thing for comparison.

A Zen master was walking on the beach with his student. "Look back," he said. "The footprints you see are your past. Look forward and imagine how your footprints might fall. That's your future. But you cannot see your present footstep. It is not possible to see the footstep you are making just now." The eyes cannot see the eyes. You can see the reflection of your eyes in the mirror, but how do you know you really have eyes and that the reflection is not an illusion? Our life unfolds without concepts. Conceptual understanding is added after the fact.

The Diamond Sutra say that past mind cannot

attain enlightenment, future mind cannot attain enlightenment, and present mind cannot attain enlightenment. What mind then can attain enlightenment? Listening is just like this. We cannot hear the sounds, cries, complaints, and yearnings of the world with past, future, or present minds. How then do we hear them?

Listen.

Mind is like the great sky. Awareness is like the great sky, containing everything, containing our aliveness, containing our energy, containing our sleepiness, containing our hopes, containing our delusions, containing our fears. Our whole life is contained in the great sky of being in this moment. This great sky has no meaning, and this *no meaning* is meaning beyond meaning, Great Meaning. Great Meaning is truth, which is compassionate action.

Awake.
All night,
sound of snowflakes.

Chapter Three

Listening and Precepts

Introduction

Buddhist precepts are guides, or pointers, for living a compassionate life. They are points of reference that enable or help us to manifest compassion in each moment. We take on precepts to support our life practice of helping others and avoiding doing harm. Yet they are difficult to take up, difficult to keep, and fraught with danger. There is the danger of not taking them seriously enough. And there is the potential danger of taking them too seriously. In Zen we teach "Know when to keep them and know when to break them." The challenge is to listen to the precepts and hear the meaning and direction behind the words.

If we don't pay careful attention, too often precepts become a standard by which we judge ourselves and others. They can become a means for measure. We can easily fall into the hell realm of using them to tell "good" from "bad." In this realm, precepts lead us to conflict and emotional violence rather than showing us a way that is free from conflict and judgment.

We can use the first five Buddhist precepts as support for listening. In fact, our practice, our pure practice, requires no precept at all. When we are functioning from our true mind, our original mind, we need no precept. We cannot break the law of Dharma when we manifest from our original mind. We have precepts for when our mind is not clear and we are not listening to the other. It is here that the precept becomes a practice of compassion.

Manifesting our original nature, bodhisattva action is unavoidable. When we listen from the mind of compassion, we need no guide. It is when we have lost our human way that signposts are needed.

First Precept: I Vow to Abstain from Taking Life

The first precept is not to kill. I vow not to kill, not to take life. Perhaps in our listening we can vow not to kill time. So when we listen, we listen fully, not wasting any time in our listening, not following any tangential irrelevancies. We listen to the core of what is being said. We vow not to be caught up in our own karma as it is stimulated by what is heard. We vow not to kill the moment.

We vow not to kill the spirit of the other with our

listening. We vow to keep our listening alive, open, and receptive, so that the spirit of the other is not harmed. When someone who is angry comes—"You don't listen to me enough!"—we will listen to that. We vow to make our listening so wide that it will include all phenomena. There is no selectivity to what we will listen to. We will not choose to listen to "this" and avoid listening to "that," just as our meditation practice does not resist any phenomenon that arises. We listen to whatever comes. No matter how unacceptable, we listen to it.

The first precept then is not to kill with our listening, not to exclude anything, not to kill time, and not to kill the phenomena of things heard. Each of us in our meditation practice has had some wild thoughts, some absolutely unexplainable thoughts. Each of us, if we've listened carefully to the inner dialogue, would be embarrassed if we had a loudspeaker on the top of our heads, broadcasting what's constantly going on inside, the checking, the chatter, the noise, the judgment, the pettiness, the criticism, the smallness. But we listen to all of it. We allow it all. We don't kill any aspect of it. We don't choose to listen to only the melodic sounds of people we care for. We listen to everyone. We listen carefully.

Killing roots out the seeds of love and mercy. To kill another is to feast on one's relatives and friends. Someday we shall be born in one of the three painful realms in payment for our killing. For it is by bestowing life that we shall receive human life in return.

Killing roots out the seeds of love and mercy. The compassion of listening is killed when our listening starts to be measured, when we begin to analyze, when we hear something being said and immediately we infer motive and cause. We add to it our translation, our interpretation, our karma, and our projections. Having been trained as a psychotherapist, I know that I can be accurate in my interpretations. But these interpretations—even when accurate—root out the seed of love and compassion and objectify the other. Even if it has some accuracy from a particular perspective, from a wider sense, it is often corrupt, toxic, and poisonous.

There are schools of psychotherapy based on analysis. Some of the neo-Freudian schools of psychoanalysis are heavily steeped in figuring out, and not trusting, the patient's process. This occurred even though Freud did very little interpretation of the patient's free associations in the consulting room. He would sit behind the patient and listen, allowing whatever came to come, not disturbing the patient's free-associative process. There is violence committed when the therapist knows more about what is being said than the one who is speaking. This is killing the other by knowing more.

We know the purity and compassion of our listening is preserved in not-knowing, in absolutely not coming to any conclusion about the other. Staying in the purity of our listening, we respond only to what is said, not adding our interpretation, our twist, our opinion about what we are listening to. Not adding karma to the process. Not adding anything.

When someone is talking in a particular way, we

may not like it. It may not be our idea of how to be intimate. But can we listen without the expectation of somebody being a certain way? Often there is resistance to this way of listening because people feel "If I don't object or offer my opinion when I disagree, people will believe that I am in agreement with them. They will think I support what they are saying even when I don't." Yet listening without judgment can be deeply healing. To be truly heard is rare and a gift beyond measure. What is resolved in the process of nonintrusive listening is outside the realm of agreement. It is a meeting that knows no limit.

I once saw a patient who was a car salesman. I saw him for several years, every week. It amazed me that he could function as well as he did in the everyday world, because the quality of his interpersonal relationship with me seemed quite limited. He would come, week after week after week, and talk about the same thing. Over and over again. During each session, we would go over the same ground again in detail, without the slightest change in content or perspective.

He had had a relationship with a woman that ended badly, and he was hurt deeply. As we would sit, there would be long silences and then he would say, "That was really something, wasn't it?" And I would say, "Yes, it was a pretty incredible relationship." And he would say, "Yeah, it was something, wasn't it?"

It would go on like this, and I would get bored, angry, and frustrated. I would try to fix it, try to psychoanalyze what the "real" problem was. I would try to figure out his pathology. I wondered if he was brain-damaged, or psychotic. These questions floated in and out of my mind. One day we were sitting in the afternoon, and as we sat, the room began to fill with the golden light of the setting sun. A golden and reddish light reflected off the side of his face in such a beautiful way. And words came out of his mouth, not with any meaning at all but like the golden beautiful words of the Buddha himself. His words flowed like the gold of the sunset pouring into the room. And I remember sitting there, sitting across from him, and experiencing how beautiful and radiant he was. Sitting across from me, he seemed to experience this, and he seemed to heal and grow. It was a moment of true friendship. It was a moment when I saw him as he was. And it arose from a stubborn persistence to just stay in the room and listen. Trusting that just sitting there, listening, was enough.

I remember sitting with another woman at a psychiatric hospital where I did an internship. She was an outpatient who came in for psychotherapy three times a week for years, perhaps ten years or more. She always wore the same dress. It was one of those light cotton dresses that mature women wear, a "kitchen" dress. I could imagine an apron around it. It was in the winter that I saw her, and she would come right on time for every visit. She would sit quietly, obediently, outside my office and wait for me. It was hot. The heat was turned up too high in my little office and I had no thermostat to adjust it. And as she did not pay too much attention to personal hygiene, I would try to open a window for some air. But the windows were painted shut after years and years of careless painting.

We would sit, and she would talk on and on end-lessly about the Lindbergh kidnapping. She even had a scrapbook, and we would go over in detail about how the child was kidnapped.

The sessions were very difficult for me. I was very sleepy. I fought sleep as she droned on and on. There were times when I wanted to go running, screaming, from the office. I never did. There were days when I felt I just could not take another rehash of the Lindbergh story; the ear cut off as evidence, the endless scrutiny of the ransom notes, the speculation about how the parents felt. There were days, many days, I hoped she wouldn't be sitting outside my door, but she almost always was. On the rare day that she would not come, I would miss her. I called to see if she was all right. She always had a legitimate reason and promised that she would be there at the next appointed time.

As I was finishing my internship at the hospital, she came in for her last appointment and brought me a card. In the card she said, "Thank you. You were the best therapist I have ever had." I was embarrassed. In my mind, I was a terrible therapist. I wasn't as interested in her as I thought I should be. I struggled constantly to be with her, to stay in the room, to not cancel her appoint-ment. I struggled desperately not to end the hour early. I felt I had done a terrible job.

Because of the long history of her illness, as well as a guarded prognosis for a full recovery, she had been to see many therapists: social workers, other psychology interns, psychiatrists doing their residency, and staff per-sonnel. She said, "You were the best therapist I have ever seen." In my complete astonishment, I said, "Why?" She said, "Because you didn't fall asleep. All the others fell asleep."

I don't know why I didn't fall asleep. I certainly fought it, biting my lip, pinching my leg. "You're going to stay awake in this warm, stuffy office, confronted with a woman who makes absolutely no sense at all." I tried. She was appreciative. I was astonished.

Second Precept: I Vow to Abstain from Taking Things Not Given

I vow to abstain from taking things not given. The taking of things not given cuts off the roots of virtue and wisdom; in attaining ease, we shall lose this ease. By merely desiring something of another, we are brought, in the future, face to face with animal rebirth.

Don't take things that are not given. We are so full of our conclusions about people that when we listen to them, we decide what they are really saying, what they really mean. We take liberties with what is heard. We all do it. "I know the truth about this one." "She says this, but she really means that." Or we begin to pry. We listen—"Oh, that's interesting"—and we pry a little deeper. "I want to hear more about that."

"No, I am interested in talking about this."

"Well, I'm really interested in that."

We pry and we try to take something. Get something out of the other. Our listening becomes intrusive, a violation. It doesn't allow the other to be who they are. We begin to force them on our terms. Our listening stops being pure, and we begin hunting, scavenging, looking around, sniffing, wondering. Not the wide wondering of pure listening, but the specific wondering of a busybody mind. Our listening follows our personal karma or mind habit rather than meeting the moment as it presents itself.

It is by bestowing life that we receive human life in return. We don't have to think of these precepts in terms of time and rebirth, of when we get a new body in a next lifetime. By listening intimately from the purity of our widest, untainted listening, we are giving life. We don't have to think of it in terms of the future. It is in this very moment that life is bestowed.

By taking something from the other, by analyzing, intruding, digging out, desiring something from the other, we are brought, in this moment, face to face with animal rebirth, animal consciousness. It is not in the future; it is right here and now that we manifest our animal nature when we take things not given.

So often when we listen to someone, we immediately reply with "I . . ." "Well, I . . ." Stealing away the other's sharing. Stealing the intimacy of something given by the other, with a personal reference. Not that referring to one's self always destroys the intimacy, breaks the bond. But if we listen carefully to ourselves, typically when someone talks and the reference becomes our experience, it means we are not listening to that person. We are comparing what is said with our own life experiences.

There are times when personal reference and sharing are not all bad. We always say about precepts: know when to keep them; know when to break them. For example, someone says to you, "I really enjoyed the concert last night. The music was absolutely wonderful." You could say, "Well, I did too. It was great. I really liked the Mozart." We want to meet the other without taking something from him. Perhaps we say, "Oh, I'm glad it made you happy. I too enjoyed it." Or sometimes just simply, "Yes." In our "yes" we cover worlds. We say "yes" to the other's enjoyment and "yes" to the fact that we enjoyed it as well. Simply and completely, "yes."

Can we take our ego out of our listening? Freud called empathy, which is therapeutic listening, a regression of the *ego* in service of the *id*. Can we see clearly that there is no self to be maintained, to be identified with, to be documented in the exchange? Can we just listen to the other? Not in a flimsy, weak way, but listening substantially and manifesting without any identification of our own, without having to allege our essence beyond the enjoyment of hearing the other? Can we just listen?

Third Precept: I Vow to Abstain from Misconduct Done in Lust

Unchastity cuts off the seed of purity.

Do we lust in our listening? Are we being seductive or seduced in our listening? Is the purity of our listening cut off? Is the intimacy, the compassion, betrayed by our needs?

Lust occurs only when we stop listening. There are times when passion can be mutually dynamic and energizing, but lust is one-sided and exploitive. It creates imbalance. When our listening is lustful, it wants something from the other. It exploits the other for its own satisfaction. "Tell me something interesting." "Entertain me." Our interest in the other can be only for pleasure. We listen only to what we want to hear. "That makes me feel good, so I want to hear more." "When you say that, I feel awful. Please stop." Or, more dramatically, "Shut up!!"

Our lustful listening usually has an ulterior motive. We listen intently because we hope our listening will bear fruit in other areas. We often want something from our listening, intimacy, approval, certain information, agreement, gratification. If we listen for personal gain of any kind, it is likely to be lustful and karma-producing. Once I was referred to a very wealthy and well-known person's daughter for psychotherapy. I was young and impressionable and thought the therapy was about me. I thought people came in to see me. How important I was, to be getting this referral. She came two or three times and never returned. She didn't even call to cancel. She just didn't show. My listening was tainted by my passion for seeing someone "important." She may not have followed through on subsequent sessions, but my *wanting* to see her in therapy obscured my ability to listen clearly and know what was going on with her.

Another example of lustful listening is what happens when two lovers listen only to each other. They hear only each other's voice. Wrapped in their feelings for each other, they cannot listen to anything else. Of course, when we meet two people who love each other, it can be enchanting. We bask in the reflection of their love. But it can easily slip into exclusivity. Lovers can easily get lost identifying with, and protecting, the feeling they get from their mate. Instead of energy that is universal and available to all, the energy gets hoarded. It becomes ego-bound and pursued for personal satisfaction and enjoyment. True love benefits all beings. It is natural, open, and nonpossessive. This is not the same as the "free love" advocated in the 1960s. This kind of "freedom" often leads to sexual acting out and self-gratification. If it is "for me"; it is not compassionate love.

Tantric sexual practices are often described as razor-edge practices. A Korean Zen master once said, "Sex is like a porcupine crawling into a rat hole." Easy to enter, difficult to back out. But there is always another way out of any tunnel; there is always an escape door. Enormous energy can be generated sexually. And if that energy is not for all beings, it will result in exclusion and suffering. Using sexual energy to benefit all beings takes meticulous attention, effort, and awareness.

For years, spiritual seekers have begged the issue of sexuality, avoiding those of the opposite sex. To avoid the issue altogether is to deny our humanness. We are sexual beings. Our sexuality may be expressed genitally with another person. Or it may be expressed by our eating or buying, or our enjoyment of the sunset or a flower. Passion is available in every sense organ. And thus, the potential for exploitation is constant. If our sense-gratification is "only for me," there is suffering. If our senses, and thus our life, are for all beings, compassion manifests in every act.

To dwell in the oneness available from intense feeling is to violate the precept against activity done in lust. Whether the oneness is from the personal samadhi that comes from intense spiritual practice, or the oneness that comes from the ego-loss available in intense interpersonal encounter, there is always the danger of delusion and attachment. Can we listen without wanting, without distorting, without grasping? Can we listen in true intimacy?

My friend Maurine Stuart Roshi used to say, "I did not become Soen Roshi's student because of the greatness of his words, although he said some marvelous things. I became his student because of the way he held his teacup."

Fourth Precept: I Vow to Abstain from Lying

I vow not to lie. I vow to speak only the truth. If our listening is functional, it will respond when someone says, "Do you like my new hairstyle?" Do we tell the truth? What is a lie? In our listening, we put aside the like-and-dislike mind and only listen to what is really being said. "I want you to be interested in me; I am interested in your interest in me." We listen to that, and we respond to that, whether we like a hairstyle, whether we like a movie, whether we like a personality. "You like my personality? I've spent several thousand dollars in psychotherapy getting it. How do you like it?" "It's okay, but you need to go back for a trim, it's a little excessive over here."

We listen to what is being said, to what is being

asked of us. We tell the truth. The truth is to not follow our karma, our liking and disliking mind, our opinions, our situation, our conditional mind. That is not the truth. The truth is not dependent on anything. The truth is exposed in some authentic contact in the moment.

"Do you like my . . . ?"

"I like being here with you, listening."

The test of truth is whether it is alive in the moment, the moment of noncomparison, of nonjudgment, of nonmeasurement. Perhaps when our listening is vital, vivid, and alive, the question "Do you like me, am I okay?" doesn't have to appear. The person is attended to so completely that he has no need for reassurance. When there is the need for reassurance, can we help the other realize his deepest value? His true self that is not dependent on anything?

> *Lying cuts off the seed of truth. Heaven does not allow deception of the saints nor lying against the holy ones.*

So often, psychotherapists start with pure intention but end up listening only for the money. They sit in the room, not because of interest but because of money and support for their needs in life. When that happens, there is burnout. A poison begins to develop. The profit-motive poison. A psychotherapy supervisor I had in graduate school used to say, "Don't trust anyone who doesn't have an alternative for making money. Only trust those who have diversified their sources of income, because they don't *have* to sit there with you."

Burnout does not come only with financial interest.

We burn out as listeners when we are stuck in our opinions. Restricted by our beliefs about what the outcome should be, we become frustrated with the way things are. Our listening becomes a wrestling match with our karma. We become tired, frustrated, and hopeless, giving up on the whole listening process.

You have only one nose, one mouth, but two ears. Why do you have two ears?

This question appears again and again. What is the direction of our listening? Why listen? To help someone with a particular problem? For power, money, fame, good feeling? When our direction is clear, then our listening is pure, without taint or lie.

Fifth Precept: I Vow to Abstain from Intoxicants, Taken to Induce Heedlessness

Liquor cuts off the roots of wisdom.

We could say that gossip cuts off the roots of wisdom. Generation after generation, we remain in a stupor as one drunk.

We intoxicate ourselves with the troubles of others, with gossip. "Did you know that . . . ?" "Have you heard . . . ?" We become deluded by it; we want more. There is an entire media industry based upon our drunkenness for information, our addiction for information about one another. We read it furiously wanting to know—what?

Can we look? Can we see how our wisdom is lost in the intoxication of gossip? It is so delicious, yet one always feels bad afterward. There is as real a hangover from a night of serious gossiping as there is from a night of serious drinking. You wake up in the morning, fuzzy-headed. All the images, pain, and self-righteousness are swimming around and around. The relationship with the other is lost. The intimacy, the purity, the immediacy, the moment-by-moment pure touching and listening with the other is lost, as you swim together in the liquor of the past and of other people's troubles.

Or one reads *Midnight* magazine or the *National Enquirer* on the way out of the supermarket. "Woman gives birth to fifteen children, pictures on page 10." "World's tiniest person, no bigger then a postage stamp." "Eight-hundred-pound woman gives birth, and didn't know she was pregnant."

And so I vow to abstain from intoxicating myself with my listening. I vow to abstain from being desirous, pursuing the gossip of things heard. Gossip destroys intimacy. To talk about another destroys the true meeting. Our time together is so brief, and we waste it gossiping.

Our gossip is so seductive, so interesting. It takes us completely out of the realm of the pure essence of our true self. We can play with a friend. Enjoy sharing stories. But to get lost, to think that it has anything to do with our life, that this story or that one, or all the gossip that we do, has absolutely anything to do with our life, is an illusion. It is a fantasy, a mistake. It betrays the moment, the pure, open, available moment that one has when talking with a friend.

And there is the intoxication of infatuation. I want to listen only to your words, be it a lover, a teacher, a guru or religious doctrine. We fall in love, or what we call love, and we want to listen only to the other. We pine for their sound when we are not with them. We compare what is heard from others with what we have heard them say. This is particularly dangerous when taking a teacher, especially charismatic teachers. We attach to their words, holding their words; we cannot hear any other teaching. Intoxicated by our teachers' teaching, we go about in a stupor, unable to hear anything else. We interpret all other teaching from the standpoint of things heard from our teachers or our religion. Our mind becomes clouded by the "truth." And thus the "truth" becomes a barrier to our hearing clearly what is in front of us.

Once there was a man who was very devout. He had lived a life of confusion and abandon but changed his ways and found God. He became quite pious, and where there was once self-consciousness and inferiority, there was now a strength and belief that was apparent in every step he took. His religion had served him well, and he was generous in his willingness to share his beliefs.

One day he was rowing a boat and came near an island. A hermit who lived on the island was praying. He heard the prayers of the hermit, and knowing as he did the true way to call God's name, he beached his boat and instructed the hermit in the correct way to pray. The hermit, grateful for the instruction, bowed, and the religious man was on his way. As he pulled away from the shore, he was joyous as he heard the hermit pray as he had instructed. But the boat was no more than a few feet off the shore when the prayers changed, and the hermit was back to his mistaken prayer forms. Disgusted, the religious man said to himself, "He is useless, he will never learn the right way to call God's name." As he looked up from his rowing, he saw, running across the water, the hermit yelling, "Sir, kind sir, how was it that I was supposed to pray God's name?"

Conclusion: I Vow Not to Give What Is Not Asked for or Not Wanted

These items might include advice, attention, interest (sexual or otherwise), psychological insight, analysis or interpretation, emotional support, understanding, confrontation, agreement, or judgments and conclusions.

To burden the other with our understandings can be worse than not listening at all. To be the "more knowing" sets up a condescension that is limiting and destructive. All psychological insight is partial and limited. Even if there is some logic to our insights, they are not truth, because truth is never partial. Expressing these fragmented insights often interferes with the speaker's process.

Once a young therapist I was supervising was talking about a male client who was having difficulty with his wife. The therapist felt the client's difficulty was due to a dysfunctional childhood relationship he had with his mother. I offered that while the therapist's insight might have merit, the client's anguish and conflict with his wife had an integrity of its own, without the insertion of a historic perspective.

There is an old story about five rabbinical students

who were huddled outside their teacher's hospital-room door. On the other side of the door, their teacher lay near death. They argued among themselves. "You go." "No, you go." Finally one of them bravely entered and said, "Rabbi, soon you will die and we will have no teacher. Please answer this one question before you die. What is the meaning of life?" The rabbi pulled the boy down and whispered in his ear, "Life is a pomegranate." "Oh," exclaimed the boy, and he ran to tell the others. "Life is a pomegranate," he announced decidedly. "Life is a pomegranate," they all said. And then the dissension began. "What does he mean, 'life is a pomegranate'? This does not make any sense. You go back in there and clarify this." The boy reluctantly went back in. "Rabbi, you said that life is a pomegranate. This does not make any sense. This 'life is a pomegranate'—no sense at all." The rabbi motioned the boy closer and whispered in his ear, "Well, maybe it isn't." And he died.

Chapter Four

Listening to a Friend

Introduction

The practice of listening is the awareness of sound as it arises, dwells, and falls away. Listening is pure and clear, not tainted by anything. Particular sounds cannot taint pure listening. Particular sounds arise, dwell, and fall away. Listening does not arise, it does not cease, and it cannot be brought about.

Original sound includes sound and no-sound. It is ever present, expressed in ten thousand forms according to circumstance. A child cries, a dying person groans, lovers moan in ecstasy—all are an expression of the one voice. It is like flour. Many kinds of foods can be made from flour: cookies, bread, cake. Flour can take many forms but is fundamentally flour, no matter what form it takes. And because flour, like sound, is not permanent or fixed, it is in constant flux, changing from a ground of emptiness.

At its basis, listening is pure emptiness. *Shunyata.* This emptiness is expressed, becomes manifest, as the unity of all sound. We refer to the manifestation of emptiness as oneness. Sometimes it is called God or Buddha-nature or the threefold body of the Tathagata or the corporal mystical body of Christ. It is the realization of this unity of all phenomena from which compassion is born. It has many names, but it cannot be spoken of or described.

When our minds are dominated by linear, discursive thought, we cannot know oneness and its root, emptiness. There is an old Hindu saying: "The mind of measure cannot know God." Once the mind has realized the fundamental ground of being, one more step is necessary. How does our realization function, moment by moment? We cannot function in the everyday world with the mind of oneness.

First, the mountain is the mountain, and the river is the river. With some realization, the mountain is the river, and the river is the mountain. Finally, when realization is complete, the mountain is blue, and the river flows down. All things are one, and yet each thing is what it is, with its particular function.

What did the Zen monk say to the hot dog vendor?

"Make me one with everything."
What did the Zen master hot dog vendor say to the
Zen monk?
"Here is your hot dog. That will be one dollar and
fifty cents, please."

From the Absolute, we listen and hear the sounds of war, the sounds of exaltation, the sounds of suffering, and the sounds of joy as an expression of the all-inclusive. And as the practice of listening becomes clear, we can listen to the color of the sky, to the smell of the pine tree, and to the feeling of a baby's soft skin. Our listening becomes so acute that we hear the flap of butterfly wings and the thunderous crash of incense falling into its dish. All are the sounds of the Universe in its purity.

We sit on the beach or on a cliff overlooking the dunes, looking out into the vast blue sky. Not a cloud appears. The waves rhythmically slap the shore. How marvelous this pure and original essence! We are embraced by the bliss of nirvana.

And yet one more step is necessary. What is the function of our enlightenment, of our realization when hearing the particular? While we realize all sound is one, we must function within particular forms. Someone comes who is hungry, what can we do? Someone comes who is crying over the loss of a loved one, how do we respond? How does our realization of the Absolute function in the particular, as the Bodhisattva Vow?

A bodhisattva is one who forgoes her own enlightenment for the sake of others, vowing to save all sentient beings before fully entering the bliss of the uncreated. The Bodhisattva Vow is "Sentient beings are numberless. I vow to save them all."

Having some experience of the bliss of emptiness, a bodhisattva does not attach to this particular state but continues to listen carefully, coming to a deep understanding of compassion and of the function of enlightenment. To attach to emptiness or to oneness is to fall into the realm of enlightenment for one's self. In Buddhism, this path is called the path of the Pratyeka Buddhas: one who listens to the teaching and realizes personal enlightenment but makes no effort to enlighten others. To dwell in one's own personal enlightenment without making the effort to help others is incomplete realization. What is incomplete inevitably leads to conflict and suffering.

It is said that if you practice hard for ten years, you will attain something. So, as is customary among many Buddhist laypeople, an old woman in China once supported a monk for ten years. She provided him with clothes and food and allowed him to live in a hermitage that she maintained. For his part, the monk only practiced very, very hard and did not have to concern himself with anything else.

After ten years, however, there was still no news from the monk. "What did he attain?" she wondered. "I must test this monk." So one afternoon, the woman summoned her eighteen-year-old daughter, who was considered one of the most beautiful young women in the village. She asked her daughter to put on makeup, her best perfume, and clothing made of the choicest material. The old woman then gave her daughter instructions for testing the monk. She sent her off to the hermitage with fine food and clothing as gifts for the monk. The woman's daughter was very excited about the plan.

When the young woman arrived at the hermitage, she bowed to the monk and said, "You have been here for ten years, so my mother made this special food and clothing for you."

"Oh, thank you very much," the monk replied. "Your mother is a great bodhisattva for supporting me like this for so long."

Hearing this, the young woman strongly embraced the monk, kissed him, and said, "How do you feel now?"

"Rotten log on cold rocks. No warmth in winter." (That is, "dwelling in complete emptiness; no feelings arise.")

Releasing him, the young woman bowed deeply and said, "You are certainly a great monk!" She returned home, full of happiness and admiration, and reported the incident to her mother. "Mother, Mother! This monk's center is very strong; his mind is not moving! He must have attained something!"

"It doesn't matter if his center is very strong, if his mind cannot be moved, or if he is a wonderful monk. What I want to know is, what did he say?"

"Oh, his words were also wonderful, Mother. He said, 'Rotten log on cold rocks. No warmth in winter.'"

"What!?" the old woman shouted. Fuming, she grabbed a big stick, ran to the hermitage, and mercilessly beat the monk, shouting, "Go away! Get out of here! I've spent ten years helping a demon!" Then she burned the hermitage to the ground.

If you were this monk, what would you do when confronted with this young woman's amorous advances?

The realization that is attained by listening always includes a wise and compassionate response. Compassion without wisdom is sentimentality. Wisdom without compassion is dry cognition. When someone comes to you with a problem and your listening is pure and clear, there is no hesitation. It is from our pure and clear listening that we know exactly what to do and say. Our listening is like a gentle rain that nourishes everything it falls on, according to need. A large plant is nourished in a large way, while a small plant is nourished in a small way. Our compassion takes its form from need. Because we dwell in the realization of the uncreated, unborn mind of no fixed self, we listen and respond, listen and respond, moment by moment, without limitation or conclusion. And our listening benefits all beings according to their need.

The Four Kinds of "Like This"

One of the ways of talking about the structure of experience, which can be applied to listening, is what Zen Master Seung Sahn calls the four kinds of "like this": "without like this," "become one like this," "like this," and "just like this."

"Without like this" describes the experience of *shunyata:* emptiness, nothingness, boundless pure space. All constructed things fall away. All conditioned things dissolve. All habits vanish in emptiness. "Without like this" is the foundation of all things, the root source of everything, complete stillness. Sitting quietly in a mountain temple, clouds disappear, ten thousand miles of clear blue sky.

"Become one like this" describes the Absolute, oneness. Emptiness is the ground of being, while oneness is the being itself. When male and female are joined, this is oneness. When mother and father are in harmony, this is the Absolute. When heaven and earth are no longer separate, the undiminished is clearly expressed. We demonstrate the Absolute with sound: *whack!!!* Everything returns to this point. The ten thousand dharmas return to one. What does the one return to? *Whack!!!*

"Like this" describes things as they are. The wall is white. The sky is blue. The tree is green. *Gong,* the sound of the bell. *Tick, tock, tick, tock,* the sound of the watch. All things as they are.

"Just like this" describes function. All phenomena have function. I am talking, you are listening.

Please listen to the following:

Here is a watch. If you say it is a watch, you are attached to name and form. If you say it isn't a watch, you are attached to emptiness. What then is it? "It is 7:30 P.M."

Here is a cup. If you say it is a cup, this stick will hit you thirty times. If you say it isn't a cup, this stick will also hit you thirty times. How do you avoid being hit? By drinking from the cup. Everything has its function. This function is expressed in its context or in what we say, in its correct situation and correct relationship.

There is a famous kong-an that Zen Master Seung Sahn created to point to correct situation, correct relationship, and correct function:

One day a man visited the Zen center. He was smoking a cigarette and blew smoke on the Buddha statue and dropped ashes on the Buddha's lap.

The abbot of the center came in and cried, "What are you doing? Are you crazy? Why are you dropping ashes on the Buddha?"

The man answered, "Don't check. Buddha is everything. So why are you attached to this statue?" The abbot was stuck and couldn't answer, so he left in frustration.

If you were the abbot, what could you do to make this situation correct? If you try to explain to the visitor the doctrine of correct function, he will only hit you because he is attached to One Mind. If you do nothing, you evade your duty to teach the proper Dharma. How do you respond?

To find your correct response to this cigarette man, you must respond to the whole situation. Your response must take in all of it. The correct response is one that reflects things as they are but also gives the exchange a direction. A clear response exposes the bone marrow of the dilemma.

A second kong-an that illustrates the point of correct function, correct relationship, and correct situation is as follows:

Three men are walking on a path. All of a sudden, one man begins to draw his sword, which makes a sound as it comes out of the scabbard. The second man waves both his hands, palms out. The third man draws a handkerchief and waves it.

If you were there, what would be *your* correct function?

The best hint to this kong-an is, it is like three people watching the same movie. One laughs at a particular scene, "Ho, ho, ho." Another laughs, "Tee-hee, tee-hee, tee-hee." And the third one laughs, "Ha, ha, ha."

While there are four kinds of "like this," these are just means of pointing at phenomena as they unfold. Each is simply a facet of the jewel of existence. It is like three men feeling an elephant. One has hold of the trunk, one has hold of the tail, and one has hold of a leg. The one who has the tail says, "Oh, this is like a rope." The one who has hold of the leg says, "No, it's like a tree." And the one who has hold of the trunk says, "You are both wrong; it's like a snake." It is not until the whole is grasped that one has a true sense of what it is, and even then, any description or explanation of it is incomplete.

Listening and the Four Kinds of "Like This"

"Without like this" is the ground of listening, complete silence. That out of which sound comes. It is spacious, vast, and empty. "Without like this" is the silence in all sound. The linear mind divides sound and silence, but sound and silence cannot be separated. Silence and sound are one. It is only with our thinking that they become separate. Can you hear the silence in the roar of the jet, in the crash of thunder, in the cry of the child?

"Become one like this" is hearing all sound as one sound, hearing all sound as the sound of the great Avalokitesvara. Every sound is the expression of the name Kwan Se Um Bosal. The wind in the trees, the crowing of a crow, the barking of a dog, are all singing

117

the name Kwan Se Um Bosal. We listen to our beloved, and his voice is the voice of the avatar of the Buddha. We listen to our friend, and our friend's voice is the marvelous nectar of Kwan Se Um Bosal. We listen to our teacher, and the sound of his voice is the sound of eternity. We listen to our students, and their sounds are the one love song of the Universe.

We make no discrimination. We are not irritated by a dog's barking. We are not frustrated by a furnace's making noise, or a car's passing. We make no judgment about the sound of our beloved's voice, whether it is in his throat or in his tandien. It is all a manifestation of the one sound. It requires no analysis or judgment. It's not *like* the sound of God; it *is* the sound of God. We don't impose an interpretation on the sound. It's not something lovely or precious to aspire to. We hear it as the sound of God, herself. That is the way it is. A fact.

Listening "like this" is to hear sound in its particular way. We don't lose our experience of the beloved, but we are not lost in the pure nectar of oneness. We hear the particular sound as it is. We don't have to analyze. The sound of the crow is just as it is. The sound of the dog is just as it is. We listen to the particular expression of the Absolute. We perceive it immediately, without any thought or special adjustment. So the "like this" of listening is simply *gong*. There is no "I am hearing the sound." There is just *gong*.

My teacher used to use the analogy, when comparing One Mind listening with Clear Mind ("like this") listening, of a student giving a piano recital. The student's mother is enraptured and only hears how wonderfully her child is playing. Her mind is one with her child's playing. She does not evaluate or discriminate. She is not listening with an ear for mistakes. The entire performance is heaven-sent. While, in contrast, the child's teacher hears every note. She hears the good, the bad, and the in-between. She hears how much pressure the child strikes the keys with, and is fully aware of her timing and pace. She listens carefully without loss of boundary. She hears it all.

The "just like this" of listening is the function of listening. What is the function of listening?

When the mind is clear, it is like a mirror. Whatever comes, the mind simply reflects it. To reflect does not mean to mimic but to correctly respond. When the traffic light turns red, we put a foot on the brake strongly enough to stop the car. When the light turns green, we look both ways and step on the gas and go, carefully watching and listening for danger. Someone comes who is angry, and we listen and respond with compassionate speech. When the mind is clear, we perceive accurately and know exactly how to respond. And when we make a mistake, we correct it and go on.

Karma and Listening

The practice of listening requires no special training. Because we are human beings, we are born listening. But because of our karma—the mind habit of lifetimes—our ability to hear without distortion or projection is obscured. To listen, and thus perceive clearly, is not a matter of adding something to the process but one of eliminating all that is not listening.

When the mind is clear, it is bright like a mirror, reflecting without contamination everything it perceives. Listening itself is curative. All problems and conflicts dissolve in the pure clear radiance of the listening moment. But sometimes when we are engaged in listening to someone, our feelings, opinions, and judgments appear.

There are two reasons for the arising of karma relative to listening. One is that what is listened to may trigger our personal karma. Deep-seated, lingering karma may come to the surface when we least expect it—as memories, fears, and expectations. Because of these reactions, we may add something to what is heard. We add interpretation, conjecture, and opinion based on our feelings. At times, this may be obvious: a gut-wrenching anxiety, anger, or the feeling or expression of some other strong emotion. Strong attraction to the speaker and strong dislike of the speaker are also indications that our karma is manifesting. And finally boredom is usually a strong indicator that we have lost the vitality of our listening and have allowed the conversation to deaden.

There is a variety of ways that karma may be expressed. We may express our karmic intrusion as a lapse in memory or as a sense of being "out of it" for a period. These states may appear, for example, when hearing about child abuse or some other difficult subject. We may also express our karma by pursuing certain topics, or by encouraging the conversation along what is interesting to us rather than what is being expressed naturally.

At other times, our karmic intrusions may not be

obvious. We may know only in retrospect that there is something happening. We may find ourselves glancing away unconsciously, or a nervous laugh may appear that even surprises us. We may drop our voice (putting the full burden of hearing onto the other) and become aware that we are doing this by the frequency of our friend's requests for repetition. Or we may inappropriately say nothing when something needs to be said, so that instead of dynamic silence, there is embarrassment. Our karma is expressed when we abruptly change the subject without knowing it or by making personal references that turn the conversation into a discussion of our life. We may find ourselves using pat phrases as a way of carrying the conversation without committing to the listening process.

It may not be clear why we have reacted with our own karma. While often it may be the content of what is heard that triggers our karmic reaction, sometimes the trigger may not be obvious. It could be a glance the speaker gives or a tone or the way he or she moves in their chair. It may be something we ate or an illness coming on. It may be an argument we have had with another, earlier in the day, that causes us to drift off into memory. It could be almost anything, and often it is not what we think it is.

A second cause for karmic reaction is what might be called borrowed karma. It is like going to a movie and being so engrossed that we identify with the characters and take on their feelings and mood. The mood and feeling from a "good" movie can last for days afterward.

Because karma has no self-nature, we listen to it. We cannot change karma, but we can be aware of it. If we are having some karmic reaction to things heard, perhaps the speaker is also experiencing something that will be revealed with a disclosure. We might respond, "When I hear you talk about that, I feel strong anger well up, and I am wondering how you feel." Or, "Listening to you tell that, I feel uncomfortable, and I imagine it bothers you also." Or we may not say anything about our own state but be guided by our reaction to listen completely and more fully. We take our distraction as impetus to be careful, to wake up, to pay close attention to what is happening. Without judgment of self or other, we listen to our reactions as well as those of our friend. We take care not to follow our karmic reaction but make an effort to stay clear. We don't try to analyze the why of the karma or impose a meaning on it. We just come back to listening again and again and again.

Listening is like other meditations in that it requires effort and focus. If, for example, one decides to meditate using the mantra "Coca-Cola," the task of the meditator is to recite "Coca-Cola" inwardly. Everything that is not "Coca-Cola" is not the meditation. So if we are saying "Coca-Cola, Coca-Cola, Coca-Cola," and the mind begins to wander, our task is to come back to "Coca-Cola." Doing the mantra "Coca-Cola" is simply that. It is not the judgment that appears about the mind's wandering or the evaluation that appears when one is distracted. There is no good or bad in the meditation. The meditation is simply "Coca-Cola, Coca-Cola." Anything that is not "Coca-Cola" is not the meditation practice that we have decided to do. Everything that is not "Coca-Cola" is let go of and we come back to "Coca-Cola."

Listening is just like this. Not evaluating our listening, not analyzing what is heard or what appears in our own consciousness, we continually come back to listening. Coming back to listening is coming back to the moment. Not going left, not going right, not going ahead, not going behind, but just listening fully, moment by moment. One can listen only in the moment. We cannot listen in the past; we cannot listen in the future; and we cannot listen in the present. Listening is a moment-by-moment phenomenon that is not dependent on time or thinking.

The continuity of karma is dependent on time. When past mind, future mind, and present mind no longer exist in the immediacy of the listening moment, how can karma persist? It is only when continuity stops that something new is possible. Thus, true creative change is not a reaction or a continuation but a possibility previously unknown. It is only from not-knowing that creativity is possible. Otherwise, we are just reorganizing the past.

Without evaluation, without self-consciousness.

Listen.

Phases of Listening

The process of listening to another can be divided into phases. Because we have the ability to think, we can examine listening from many different perspectives. We can understand listening as a process that has a beginning, a middle, and an end. We can make categories about listening and separate a speaker from a hearer. Although sometimes it is useful in our listening practice to devise arbitrary phases and categories, we know that this devising is only *upaya,* skillful means. Listening is only listening. No beginning, middle, or end. No hearer and nothing to hear.

For many years, I taught psychotherapists in training. We would look at the listening process in terms of its impact on the speaker. The first phase is considered the foundation phase. It is the phase where rapport and "communication" are established. Not to develop rapport or foundation for the listening can cause problems for both the listener and the speaker. To give advice too early in the process, or not to respond fully to the other, can cause further suffering. I have heard it said in the Tibetan tradition that if a teacher gives a teaching before its time, he will be turned to charcoal. We all have certainly experienced the heat when we have missed others with our comments or remarks to things they have said. There are some individuals who are charismatic, and their very presence establishes a base for listening. At least in the beginning, it is best not to rely on personal charisma to carry the first phase.

Once we have established a base or "connection" with the speaker by listening and communicating back that we have heard what was said, the next function of our listening is to respond, revealing a clear direction for the encounter. We give direction to what was said by responding not only to what was heard on the surface but to all the implications of what was heard. Thus, direction arises directly from phenomenon itself and is revealed by our clarity and skillful means in responding to it. Hearing one thing, we respond to the many.

In every listening encounter, there is what is heard, just as it was said without any intervention. But our listening becomes dynamic when it includes a response to what is heard. Sometimes the response is silence, allowing others to dwell on what they have said. This is oftentimes the most difficult response because it seems like no response. Social convention requires us to be polite and say something when indeed the best response may be no response. Sometimes the response is simply a reflection of what is said. And sometimes our response is a "turning phrase" that allows for a deeper awareness of the phenomenon and clarifies the direction of what is heard. Seeing the horns, we respond to the ox.

The following are five somewhat arbitrary divisions of listening:

Attention

Primary in listening is attention.

A student said to the master, "Master, what is the true Dharma?" The master writes, "Attention." The student persists, "Only this? Only attention?" The master writes again, "Attention." "Okay, I understand attention. But what else?" And the master writes a third time, "Attention."

So attention is the beginning, the middle, and the end. Just attend to the moment. Suffering appears, and there is a tendency to separate oneself from it. Not my suffering; her suffering, his suffering, their suffering. We try to live in a cocoon of good feeling and well-being.

Our comfort-needs tend to muffle our awareness and attention to suffering.

It is a fact that we, as human beings, are not as attentive as we need to be. The fact that all suffering is not separate from us is difficult to realize. But when one suffers, all suffer. When suffering appears, it requires some response. When someone comes into our life who is suffering, bringing a problem, how is it that we don't attend?

When someone comes, the first step is to find a place where there is little distraction. It can be difficult to give undivided attention when there is music in the background or people talking. Perhaps the first step is to go somewhere safe and comfortable that supports our attention. If someone comes whose primary need is physical hunger, it can be difficult to listen to him and his complaint about his wife, or her husband, or children or job. Even though we hear the words, the situation requires deep attention. When someone comes who is hungry, giving him or her some food is our teaching. Attending to another is to know what "food" is necessary. It would not be too productive to talk to a baby whose stomach is swollen with starvation. To soothe it with words would be missing the mark.

Yet there are pitfalls in our attention. Oftentimes people come who are quite needy, wanting, hungry. To feed their emotional needs may only create dependence. To give "correct" attention is to avoid responding to what is at the surface and to clearly see what is needed.

Typically, one responds to hunger by feeding it, not because it is appropriate but because of the discomfort one feels in hearing the hunger of another. We are trying to overcome *our* discomfort, *our* hunger, not the hunger of the other. It is like children who are crying. There are times when you give them something, but it is also important for them to be frustrated and not always get what they want. This helps to build a sense of character and integrity. It will happen anyway because we cannot provide for others everything that they need. In fact, we can provide very little for another. So it will happen that they will come up against wanting and not getting. How can we as listeners respond so that others can get what they need, without creating a debilitating dependency?

Sam, my son, at age six wanted an oven that bakes rubber figures. He wanted it for weeks. It was a constant cry, a constant suffering. He tried to get someone to take him to the store, tried to get the money for it. He was insistent, demanding, throwing himself on the ground, packing a bag and walking out of the house. Neither his mother nor I would get it for him. It became the most important thing to him. What was interesting was to watch his resourcefulness appear out of his frustration. Getting something he didn't have became quite a project for him. Finally he got it. He paid for it on his own by doing chores and earning the money.

In contrast, Sam's best friend invited him to go to Gatlinburg, Tennessee, for two nights. And not only was his "best" friend going but his older "best" friend was going as well. It was absolutely the most fantastic idea that he could think of, to go to Gatlinburg with his two friends over two nights. And he asked me if he could go. I said "Of course not, you cannot go." And he threw a fit, fell on the floor. He would wake up in the morning, and it would be the first thing on his lips, "Dad, why can't I go?" Sam has attempted to spend the night at a friend's house before and would come home in the middle of the night. It is quite a long drive from Gatlinburg, six hours.

There were other issues that I was concerned about. The older boys who were going had a tendency to pick on the younger boys. My guess is he could have gone, but I felt he wasn't ready. So there was frustration and attending to that. And what he began to realize from my attention to him as we talked about it was the fact that he hadn't spent the night at anyone's house successfully and the fact that an older boy was going who tended to get tired of him because of the age difference. And as older boys often do when they get bored with younger friends, he would pick on Sam and make his life uncomfortable. Gatlinburg was a long way away, which was also hard for Sam to understand. I could see Sam's hesitation growing. In paying attention, Sam also heard his hesitation, and it was awareness of that hesitation that allowed him to let go.

In both cases Sam was frustrated. In the first case, attention to this frustration revealed a resourcefulness. In the second case, attention to the frustration revealed awareness of what was unspoken and denied.

It is in attention that one learns how to respond to the pain and frustration of the one in need. It is in attention that one learns what will be too much, what is not enough, and what can't be helped.

So attention is the first point of listening. Hearing, knowing the other. Not understanding the other, but knowing in a deep way. Perceiving exactly what is there.

The puppy is whimpering outside the door. Don't kill it with kindness.

Hear What Is Said

Once we have paid attention, the second point in listening is hearing what is said. Truly hearing what is said. Neither adding nor taking away in our hearing, in our listening. Listen to what is said. Most of us quickly contaminate what is said. Something is said, and we come to some conclusion about it. Immediately we draw some conclusion. If we are a sophisticated psychotherapist, our conclusions may be steeped in psychoanalytic, Gestalt, Kaizerian, Mauerian, or Eriksonian interpretation. Our conclusions are steeped in some professional theory. But they are conclusions nonetheless. If we are involved with this person in a way to get our own needs met, we begin to hear the other in terms of our own needs. We come to conclusions about what is said that are based on our needs. We don't hear the other. We don't allow the other's words or expressions to stand alone as they are. There is contamination by opinion.

Our teaching is "Put down your opinion, your condition, your situation. Put down your small 'I.'" That's the meaning of true listening. You cannot hear the bird sing, the dog bark, the friend's suffering; you cannot hear where the other is if you are listening to your own condition, opinion, and situation. Our condition is suffering. We cannot hear the cries and suffering of the world when we are fixated on our own suffering. We hear only our own projections, our own imaginations, our own speculations, our own distortions, our own pain.

Respond to What Is Heard

After we have heard what is said, the third point is to respond. Can we respond in such a way so as to neither add nor subtract?

A common mistake listeners make when responding is to respond with "I."

Having heard the other, we often take the reference back to ourselves. "Well, I . . ." "When I . . . " "That's not my experience." Can we respond to the other without self-reference?

Once a monk asked a Zen master, "What is the Truth?"

The master said, "Listen."

The student replied, "You say, 'listen,' but I cannot hear it."

The master answered, "You have 'I,' so you cannot hear."

"Do you hear it?" the student asked.

The master answered, "If you make 'I,' you cannot hear, but if you make 'you,' it is even more difficult to hear."

When we're listening from a mind that is clear, speech that comes from our mouth is not egocentric speech. It is not the delusive speech of self-centeredness. When our listening is pure, we can't help but be compassionate. If we come from the point of listening itself, we don't have to adjust ourselves in any special way. If we listen and are fully present, our karmic patterns fall away. And thus falls away all destructive or hurtful speech, our conditioning, our habits, and negative thoughts.

Perceive the Deepest Meaning of What Is Heard

The next point is perceiving what is deeply said. Hearing and responding at the deepest level. Not responding to what is apparent, but hearing the whole of it. What is said is always the tip of the iceberg. Knowing the depth and breadth of ice underneath the water's surface takes clarity and integrity on the part of the listener. There are no theories one can rely on or structures outside of the wisdom that comes with clear listening. Often out of insecurity, the listener will rely on some system to interpret things heard. To perceive at the deepest levels requires a courage of not-knowing that is rarely comfortable or predictable. It is seeing the horns and knowing there is a bull. Hearing one thing and knowing many. It is true empathy.

The kong-an for this particular level of listening is the Nam Cheon's Cat kong-an. The monks in the east village and the monks in the west village were fighting over a cat. "I want the cat." "No, I want the cat." "No, I want the cat. It is our cat." "No, it's our cat."

Nam Cheon, the famous Zen master, grabbed the cat by its tail, took out a sword, and said to the assembled monks, "If you can say one word, I will not kill the cat. If one monk can come forward and say one word, the cat is free." At that time, no monk came forward, and Nam Cheon cut the cat in two.

Later that day, Joju, who had been away during the incident, came back and Nam Cheon told him the story. After telling the story, he asked Joju, "If you were there, what would you have done?" Joju put his shoes on top of his head, turned, and walked away. Nam Cheon yelled after him, "Had you been there, you would have saved the cat!"

Passing this kong-an is to truly perceive what is going on at the deepest levels. Attaining this kong-an is to be able to truly respond to what is perceived. It is not enough to simply understand this kong-an and come up with a good response. This kong-an is our life, and we must attain it completely in every pore of our body, in every moment of our life. It is the fundamental expression of this human life.

Responding to the deepest expression of the other person may not require much. Sometimes a simple touch is enough. Sometimes a bowl of soup. Sometimes simply silence. We've heard it said that there was a man with a gun pointed at another. A Zen master, quite a distance away, saw this and shouted at just the right moment, in just the right way. The gun dropped. The person hesitated, and a life was saved.

A monk came to Joju and said, "For many years I have heard about the stone bridge at Joju Mountain. But having come here, I see only an ordinary log bridge."

Joju reflected, "You only see the log bridge. You do not see the stone bridge."

The monk revealed more. "Where is the stone bridge?"

Joju replied, "Horses cross, asses cross."

Responding with Direction at the Deepest Level

Finally, after we've attended, heard, responded, and perceived, what direction does the encounter take?

In true listening with direction, there is no opinion, no condition, no situation—only listening and hearing the deepest level. True love is the empty mirror, the meeting.

Ryokan was a monk and poet, a beautiful man, innocent beyond compare. He used to play with the children while he was in town begging. One day he was playing hide-and-go-seek with the children, and he was hiding in the outhouse. All the children got together and decided to play a trick on him, so they took off and went home. Ryokan stayed all afternoon and all night in the outhouse. In the morning, an old woman came to use the outhouse. "Ryokan," she cried, "what are you doing here?" He looked up and placed his fingers to his lips and said, "Don't tell the children!"

Ryokan had a wide, innocent mind. Walking home one day after begging, he had some coins and wondered why people were so happy when they found money. He threw his money on the ground and picked it up. "This is strange," he thought. "I'm not happy." He dropped his money again and picked it up again. He dropped his money a third time, but this time he was a little careless and lost some of it in the grass. He began to look around desperately for it. "Oh, now I understand!" Simple mind.

Once Ryokan was invited to his brother's house. His nephew was misbehaving. Knowing of Ryokan's saintly quality and his magnificent rapport with children, his brother invited him for dinner. The sole purpose of his visit was to encourage his nephew to get over whatever it was that was troubling him. The brother had hoped that Ryokan would talk with the boy, straighten him out, fix him. Ryokan came and had dinner and didn't say a word to the boy. He went to bed that night and still hadn't said a word. The brother and his wife were wondering whether Ryokan was going to talk to their son. When it was time for Ryokan to leave, the boy, acting according to custom in Japan, knelt down and tied the shoes of his uncle, and then he felt something warm and wet on his neck. When he lifted up his head, he saw tears falling from the eyes of his uncle. Not a word was spoken, but from then on the boy changed.

Ryokan truly listened to the boy and was able to respond from his heart to the boy's heart. Ryokan was not reprimanding the boy but truly felt the boy's unhappiness, and reflected it with his tears. Knowing the sadness that is behind all anger, the unhappiness that is the basis for all acting out, Ryokan teaches us how to respond with the deepest level of empathy.

Chapter Five

Repaying an Old Debt

One day, Zen Master Man Gong and some of his students were eating watermelon at Po Dak Sah. Man Gong announced to everyone, "If you can bring me the sound of the cicada, you don't have to pay for the watermelon today. If you cannot bring me the sound, you must pay for the watermelon." One monk made a sound with his mouth, imitating a cicada. Another monk made a circle on the ground and, sitting in the center, said, "In form, no Buddha; in Buddha, no form." And another monk pretended to move like a cicada.

Many monks and laypeople gave many different answers, but Man Gong would only say, "You, too, have to pay for the watermelon." Finally one monk came forward and gave Man Gong the correct answer. Man Gong smiled, bowed, and said, "You understand. Here is your watermelon."

If you were at the picnic that day with Zen Master Man Gong, how would you answer him? What was the response Man Gong was looking for?

"If you can bring me the sound of the cicada, you don't have to pay for the watermelon." This is our life. "If you please me, if you make me happy, if you do what is expected, what I expect, then somehow your life will be easier." This is what we all learn in childhood. If you do this, if you obey authority—whether the authority is within a marriage context, whether the authority lies in some institution, whether the authority is that of some religious hierarchy, whether the authority is simply within your job—"If you do and behave the way we want you to, you'll have some freedom, some advantage here." And we live in a world of resentment and anger, being led around by our noses, or chasing after carrots on a stick. Even if we happen to get a bite of the carrot, we are still hungry.

This is not to say that opposition to authority is the path to freedom either. To oppose authority, or react against it, is the same as following it—same coin, different sides. But in every situation, listen carefully; and in every situation, at every point, there is a clear and definite action. Everything we do, even something as simple as lifting a teacup to our lips, can be done without contingencies, without dependence on anything.

Kyong Ho Sunim, who was a very famous sutra-master and the seventy-fifth patriarch in the Chogye Order in Korea and now in America (the Kwan Um School of Zen lineage of Zen masters), went to visit his first teacher. He was traveling on foot and came upon a village where there seemed to be no people. He went into house after house and found dead corpses decomposing in every dwelling. He was frightened and confused by what he saw. Finally he came upon a sign that said "IF YOU VALUE YOUR LIFE, GO AWAY, CHOLERA" in big bold red letters. The sign struck Kyong Ho Sunim's mind. "I am a great sutra-master, yet I am still attached to this human form." Even though he understood that life and death are not separate, he was afraid and hindered by his fear. On his way back to the temple, his mind was seized by this great paradox.

When he got back to the temple, he summoned all his students and told them that he was going into seclusion. He told them, "I am a sutra-master and have learned the Buddha's words, but I have not attained the Buddha's mind. Even though I understand Buddhism, I have not attained true understanding." He sent them away to study with other teachers and stayed in his room day and night, meditating, for three months. He vowed not to leave his room until he realized the truth of "no life and no death." All day and night he practiced Zen, either sitting or lying down but never sleeping. It is said that he worked with the kong-an "Before the donkey leaves, the horse has already arrived."

One devoted student stayed with him, bringing him food. One day, while the attendant was in town begging for food, he met a layman who was a close friend of Kyong Ho Sunim.

The layman asked, "How is Kyong Ho Sunim these days?"

The student responded, "These days he is doing very hard training. He only eats, sits, and lies down."

"Well, if he just eats, sits, and lies down, he will be reborn a cow," the layman responded.

"Oh!! You are wrong," the attendant shouted. "He is a great teacher, and I am sure he will go to Heaven after he dies."

The layman corrected the student and said, "That is not the way to answer."

"Please teach me. How should I have answered?" asked the student.

"If he is reborn a cow, he will be a cow with no nostrils," responded the layman. "Go tell your teacher this."

The student raced back to the temple to tell Kyong Ho Sunim what happened. After hearing the story of this encounter from his student, Kyong Ho Sunim burst into laughter. His eyes bright and blazing, he threw open the doors and came out of his room.

He wrote the following poem:

I heard about the cow with no nostrils
and suddenly the whole universe is my home.
Yon Am Mountain lies flat under the road.
A farmer at the end of his work is singing.

Soon after this, he received transmission from Zen Master Man Hwa. Zen Master Man Hwa named him *Kyong Ho,* which means "empty mirror."

When we meet, whether in sadness, joy, fear, ambivalence, or expectation, how do we respond? If we try to please, avoid, or placate, then true meeting is lost. Not responding out of habit, not being pulled by the nose-ring in our nostrils, can we meet head-on, eyebrow to eyebrow? Can we listen, without the formation of a reactive self that arises from the conditioned mind of thought?

Man Gong says, "If you can bring me the sound of the cicada, you won't have to pay for the watermelon. You get the watermelon for free, if you bring me the sound of the cicada." And so we listen to the sound of the cicada. We listen to it completely. We dwell in the sound of the cicada. We sit there and become one with the sound of the cicada. We spend a lifetime listening. Clearly listening. And then the dilemma: how does one bring that sound to another? How does one manifest realization of the sound of the cicada in a way that the other can receive it? It can't be mimicked; one can't pretend. How then can one authentically manifest whatever realization is attained, dwelling fully on the sound of the cicada? How does listening manifest in a way that completely and totally touches Zen Master Man Gong?

If we attach to the sound of the cicada, we can never be free. If we attach to pleasing Man Gong, we will never be free. If we break free of everything, even the idea of freedom, there is realization that "just this!" is the source of all existence. Everything is contained in this.

How does one manifest in every situation as the Source, completely, without contingency? This is the dilemma in everything we do, whether we're married, whether we're a monk, whether we're in school, whether we're working on a job. How to act, swiftly, clearly, and directly?

"If you can bring me the sound of the cicada, you don't have to pay for the watermelon." On that day, many monks and many people brought Man Gong an answer, and all of them were wrong. But one monk came with an answer, and Man Gong bowed deeply and said, "You understand my mind."

It is not difficult to take refuge in the Dharma, to realize that the Dharma is nothing more than that which is just now sitting here, listening. There is only right here, right now, from just where you are, that you are able to act. There is no Dharma or truth outside of this. It is simply a fact. Listen and discover. Where else would you act from, if not here, not now? Where else, at what point, would your life unfold if not here, if not now from this moment?

The jewel of the Dharma, all there is, is this moment, this clear and present moment. And if this moment is lived fully, without hesitation, then all of life will unfold without hindrance. Right now, with this particular energy-vortex spinning through us, perhaps we have some sense of this. But later, with the distractions of driving the car, sitting down at the table, going to work and to school, it will seem like a dream, like an illusion. Soon there will be the question "Why practice Zen at all?"

And yet, in this moment, in perfect clarity, we realize that there is nothing but the pure Dharma jewel.

Is it possible to listen, truly listen, and not compromise listening in hope for the other? Not compromising listening for fear that what is said or expressed won't be heard?

True listening is listening from the reality that there is no enduring self. Not only from the point of view of Dharma is there no persistent self, but also from the point of view of karma there is no self that endures. From the point of view of truth, self is impermanent and illusions have no self-nature. The thinking mind wants a permanent self in everything that is done, everything said, everything smelled, everything heard, everything tasted, everything touched, and in all thoughts. There is longing for permanence, constancy, and continuity. Yet in spite of this longing, everything is reborn, new in each moment.

But there is one thing that is "permanent," unborn, uncreated, unconditioned. There is one thing that never changes and is dependent on nothing. Listen to it. Just completely listen. To truly understand is to listen completely. Hearing it all, not being identified with the content of it for even one second. Just listening without conclusion or conjecture. When listening to pain, only AH! Holding onto nothing. Realizing there is nothing to hold on to. Listen. Don't oppose listening. Just listen to it all, and compassionate action will result. When one listens to the cicada without any gaining idea, one knows exactly how to get the watermelon, and how to help others get watermelon is also perfectly clear.

Thank you for listening.

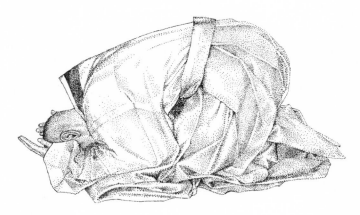

Appendix 1

The Great Dharani (Korean)

shin-myo jang-gu dae-da-ra-ni
na-mo-ra da-na da-ra ya-ya
na-mak ar-ya ba-ro-gi-je sae-ba-ra-ya
mo-ji sa-da-ba-ya
ma-ha sa-da-ba-ya
ma-ha ga-ro-ni-ga-ya
om sal-ba-ba-ye su da-ra-na
ga-ra-ya da-sa-myong
na-mak-ka-ri-da-ba
i-mam ar-ya ba-ro-gi-je
sae-ba-ra da-ba i-ra-gan-ta .
na-mak ha-ri-na-ya ma-bal-ta
i-sa-mi sal-bal-ta sa-da-nam

su-ban a-ye-yom sal-ba bo-da-nam
ba-ba-mar-a mi-su-da-gam da-nya-ta

om a-ro-gye a-ro-ga
ma-ji-ro-ga ji-ga-ran-je
hye-hye-ha-rye ma-ha mo-ji sa-da-ba
sa-ma-ra sa-ma-ra ha-ri-na-ya
gu-ro-gu-ro gal-ma sa-da-ya sa-da-ya
do-ro-do-ro mi-yon-je
ma-ha mi-yon-je da-ra da-ra
da-rin na-rye sae-ba-ra ja-ra-ja-ra
ma-ra-mi-ma-ra a-ma-ra
mol-che-ye hye-hye ro-gye sae-ba-ra
ra-a mi-sa-mi na-sa-ya
na-bye sa-mi sa-mi na-sa-ya
mo-ha ja-ra mi-sa-mi
na-sa-ya ho-ro-ho-ro ma-ra-ho-ro
ha-rye ba na-ma-na-ba
sa-ra sa-ra shi-ri shi-ri
so-ro so-ro mot-cha mot-cha
mo-da-ya mo-da-ya
mae-da-ri-ya ni-ra-gan-ta
ga-ma-sa nal-sa-nam
ba-ra-ha-ra-na-ya
ma-nak-sa-ba-ha
shit-ta-ya sa-ba-ha
ma-ha-shit-ta-ya sa-ba-ha
shit-ta-yu-ye sae-ba-ra-ya sa-ba-ha
ni-ra-gan-ta-ya sa-ba-ha
ba-ra-ha mok-ka shing-ha
mok-ka-ya sa-ba-ha

ba-na-ma ha-ta-ya sa-ba-ha
ja-ga-ra yok-ta-ya sa-ba-ha
sang-ka som-na-nye mo-da-na-ya sa-ba-ha
ma-ha-ra gu-ta da-ra-ya sa-ba-ha
ba-ma-sa gan-ta i-sa-shi che-da
ga-rin-na i-na-ya sa-ba-ha
mya-ga-ra jal-ma ni-ba
sa-na-ya sa-ba-ha na-mo-ra
da-na-da-ra ya-ya na-mak ar-ya
ba-ro gi-je sae-ba-ra-ya
sa-ba-ha

Appendix 2

Morning Bell Chant (Korean)

won-cha jong-song byon bop-kye
chor-wi yu-am shil gae myong
sam-do i-go pa do-san
il-che jung-saeng song jong-gak
na-mu bi-ro gyo-ju
hwa-jang ja-jon
yon bo-gye ji gum-mun po nang-ham ji ok-chuk
jin-jin hon ip
chal-chal wol-lyung
ship-cho ku-man o-chon sa-ship-pal-cha
il-sung won-gyo
na-mu dae-bang-gwang bul hwa-om gyong
na-mu dae-bang-gwang bul hwa-om gyong

na-mu dae-bang-gwang bul hwa-om gyong
je-il gye
yag-in yong-nyo-ji
sam-se il-che bul
ung gwan bop-kye song
il-che yu shim jo
pa-ji-ok jin-on
na-mu a-tta shi-ji-nam sam-myak
sam-mot-ta gu-chi-nam
om a-ja-na ba-ba ji-ri ji-ri hum
na-mu a-tta shi-ji-nam sam-myak
sam-mot-ta gu-chi-nam
om a-ja-na ba-ba ji-ri ji-ri hum
na-mu a-tta shi-ji-nam sam-myak
sam-mot-ta gu-chi-nam
om a-ja-na ba-ba ji-ri ji-ri hum
won a jin-saeng mu byol-lyom
a-mi-ta bul dok sang su
shim-shim sang gye ok-ho gwang
yom-nyom bul-li gum-saek sang
a jip yom-ju bop-kye gwan
ho-gong wi-sung mu bul gwan
pyong-dung sa-na mu ha cho
gwan-gu so-bang na-mu so-bang dae-gyo-ju a-mi-ta
mu-ryang su yo-rae bul
na-mu a-mi-ta bul (seven times)
chong-san chop-chop mi-ta-gul
chang-he mang-mang jong-myol gung
mul-mul yom-nae mu gae-ae
ki-gan song-jong hak-tu hong

na-mu a-mi-ta bul
san-dan jong-ya jwa mu-on
jok-chong nyo-yo bon ja-yon
ha-sa so-pung dong-nim ya
il-song han-ang-nyu jang-chon
na-mu a-mi-ta bul
won gong bop-kye jae jung-saeng
dong-im-mi-ta dae won-hae
jin mi-rae je-do jung saeng
ja-ta il-shi song bul-do
na-mu a-mi-ta bul
na-mu so-bang jong-to gung-nak se-gye
sam-shim-nyung-man-ok il-shib-il-man
gu-chon-o-baek dong-myong dong-ho
dae-ja dae-bi a-mi-ta bul
na-mu so-bang jong-to gung-nak se-gye
bul-shin jang-gwang
sang-ho mu-byon gum-saek-kwang-myong
byon-jo bop-kye
sa-ship par-won do-tal jung-saeng
bul-ga-sol bul-ga-sol-chon
bul-ga-sol hang-ha-sa bul-chal mi-jin-su
do mak-chug-wi mu-han guk-su
sam-baeng-nyuk-shi-man-ok
il-shib-il-man gu-chon-o-baek
dong myong dong-ho dae-ja dae-bi
a-dung do-sa kum-saek yo-rae
na-mu a-mi-ta bul (five times)
bon-shim mi-myo jin-on da-nya-ta
om a-ri da-ra sa-ba-ha (three times)

Morning Bell Chant (English)

Our vow:
May the sound of this bell
spread throughout the universe,
make all the hell of dark metal bright,
relieve the three realms of suffering,
shatter the hell of swords,
and bring all beings to enlightenment.
Homage to the shining, loving, holy one,
the great master Vairocana, Buddha of Light.
Now we recite the treasured verse from the golden book
and display the jeweled box with the jade axle.
Each particle of dust interpenetrates every other one.
Moment by moment, each is perfectly complete.
One hundred million, ninety-five thousand, forty-eight
    words
are the complete teaching of the one vehicle.

Homage to the great, wide Buddha: the Flower
Ornament Sutra

The first verse:
If you wish to understand thoroughly
all Buddhas past, present, and future,
you should view the nature of the universe
as created by mind alone.

The mantra of shattering hell:
Na-mu a-ta shi-ji nam sam-yak
sam-mo-ta gu-chi-nam
om a-ja-na ba-ba ji-ri ji-ri hum (three times)

We vow for our entire life to keep our minds,
without distraction, on Amita Buddha,
the Buddha of infinite time and space.
All minds are forever connected to this jade brightness.
No thought ever departs from this golden form.
Holding beads, perceiving the universe;
with emptiness as the string,
there is nothing unconnected.

Perceive and attain the western Amita Buddha.
Become one with the great western master,
the "just like this" Buddha of infinite life.
Become one: infinite time, infinite space Buddha.

The blue mountain of many ridges is the Buddha's
        home.
The vast ocean of many waves is the palace of stillness.
Be with all things without hindrance.
Few can see the crane's red head atop the pine tree.
Become one: infinite time, infinite space Buddha.

Sitting quietly in a mountain temple in the quiet night,
extreme quiet and stillness is original nature.
Why then does the western wind shake the forest?
A single cry of winter geese fills the sky.
Become one: infinite time, infinite space Buddha.

Vowing openly with all world beings,
entering together Amita's ocean of great vows,
continuing forever to save sentient beings,
you and I simultaneously attain the way of Buddha.
Become one: infinite time, infinite space Buddha.

Become one with the western pure land,
a world of utmost bliss.
The thirty-six billion, one hundred nineteen thousand,
five hundred names of the Buddha are all the same
      name.
Great Love, great compassion, Amita Buddha.
Become one with the western pure land,
a world of utmost bliss.

This Buddha's body is long and wide.
This auspicious face is without boundary
and this golden color shines everywhere,
pervading the entire universe.

Forty-eight vows to save all sentient beings.

No one can say, nor say its opposite.
No one can say, because Buddha is like
the Ganges's innumerable grains of sand
or the infinite moments in all time
or innumerable dust particles
or countless blades of grass,
numberless number.

The three hundred sixty billion,
one hundred nineteen thousand,
five hundred names of the Buddha are all the same
      name.

Great love, great compassion, our original teacher.

Homage to the golden Tathagata Amita Buddha.
Become one: infinite time, infinite space Buddha.

The mantra of original mind's sublimity:
Om a-ri da-ra sa-ba-ha (3 times)

Appendix 3

Heart Sutra (Korean)

ma-ha ban-ya ba-ra-mil-ta shim gyong
kwan-ja-jae bo-sal haeng shim ban-ya
ba-ra-mil-ta shi jo-gyon o-on gae gong
do il-che go-aek
sa-ri-ja saek-pur-i-gong
gong-bur-i-saek saek-chuk-shi-gong
gong-juk-shi-saek
su-sang-haeng-shik yok-pu-yo-shi
sa-ri-ja shi-je-bop-kong-sang
bul-saeng-bul-myol bul-gu-bu-jong
bu-jung-bul-gam shi-go gong-jung-mu-saek
mu su-sang-haeng-shik mu an-i-bi-sol-shin-ui

mu saek-song-hyang-mi-chok-pop
mu-an-gye nae-ji mu-ui-shik-kye

mu-mu-myong yong mu-mu-myong-jin
nae-ji mu-no-sa yong-mu-no-sa-jin
mu go-jim-myol-to mu-ji yong-mu-dug-i
mu-so duk-ko bo-ri-sal-ta ui
ban-ya ba-ra-mil-ta go-shim-mu gae-ae
mu-gae-ae-go mu-yu-gong-po
wol-li jon-do mong-sang gu-gyong yol-ban
sam-se je-bur-ui ban-ya
ba-ra-mil-ta go-dug-a-nyok-ta-ra
sam-myak sam-bo-ri go-ji ban-ya
ba-ra-mil-ta shi dae-shin-ju
she dae-myong-ju shi mu-sang-ju
shi mu-dung-dung ju nung je il-che go
jin-shil bur-ho go-sol ban-ya ba-ra-mil-ta
ju juk-sol-chu-wal
a-je a-je ba-ra-a-je ba-ra-sung-a-je mo-ji sa-ba-ha
a-je a-je ba-ra-a-je ba-ra-sung-a-je mo-ji sa-ba-ha
a-je a-je ba-ra-a-je ba-ra-sung-a-je mo-ji sa-ba-ha
ma-ha ban-ya ba-ra-mil-ta shim gyong

The Heart Sutra (English)

The Maha Prajna Paramita Hrdaya Sutra

Avalokitesvara Bodhisattva,
when practicing deeply the Prajna Paramita,
perceives that all five skandhas are empty
and is saved from all suffering and distress.

"Shariputra,
form does not differ from emptiness;
emptiness does not differ from form.
That which is form is emptiness;
that which is emptiness form.

"The same is true of feelings,
perceptions, impulses, consciousness.

"Shariputra,
all dharmas are marked with emptiness;
they do not appear or disappear,
are not tainted or pure,
do not increase or decrease.

"Therefore, in emptiness no form, no feelings,
perceptions, impulses, consciousness.

"No eyes, no ears, no nose, no tongue, no body,
        no mind;
no color, no sound, no smell, no taste, no touch,
no object of mind;
no realm of eyes
and so forth until no realm of mind consciousness.
No ignorance and also no extinction of it,
and so forth until no old age and death
and also no extinction of them.
No suffering, no origination,
no stopping, no path, no cognition,
also no attainment with nothing to attain.

The Bodhisattva depends on Prajna Paramita
and the mind is no hindrance;

without any hindrance no fears exist.
Far apart from every perverted view one dwells in
    Nirvana.

"In the three worlds
all buddhas depend on Prajna Paramita
and attain Anuttara Samyak Sambodhi.

"Therefore, know that Prajna Paramita
is the great transcendent mantra,
is the great bright mantra,
is the utmost mantra,
is the supreme mantra,
which is able to relieve all suffering
and is true, not false.
So proclaim the Prajna Paramita mantra,
proclaim the mantra which says:
gate, gate, paragate, parasamgate, bodhi svaha,
gate, gate, paragate, parasamgate, bodhi svaha
gate, gate, paragate, parasamgate, bodhi svaha!"

About the Author

Zen Master Dae Gak, an ordained monk, is a dharma heir of Zen Master Seung Sahn. He received *Inka* in April 1988 and final Transmission in July 1994. He has studied Zen since 1969 in both Japanese and Korean traditions.

Dae Gak Sunim established The Lexington Zen Center in 1980, which led to the founding of Furnace Mountain in 1986. Furnace Mountain is a Zen residential community located on 600 acres of woodland in rural Kentucky. Under the direction of Dae Gak Sunim, a traditional Zen temple, Kwan Se Um Sang Ji Sah, was built and opened in August 1994.

For the past six years, Dae Gak Sunim has taught internationally. He is the Guiding Teacher of centers in the United States and Australia. He also leads a yearly

Christian-Zen retreat at the Abbey of Gethsemani, the Catholic monastery in Bardstown, Kentucky.

Zen Master Dae Gak holds a Ph.D. in clinical psychology and has been a practicing psychotherapist since 1968.